The
Family Herbal
Cookbook

Cecilia Tan

TIMES EDITIONS

For this book, the publisher wishes to thank **Sia Huat Private Limited** for the loan and use of their tableware.

Managing Editor   : Jamilah Mohd Hassan
Editor   : Selina Kuo
Art Direction/Designer   : Geoslyn Lim
Photographer   : Charlie Lim
Food Stylist   : Sharon Soh
Production Co-ordinator : Nor Sidah Haron

Published by Times Editions – Marshall Cavendish
An imprint of Marshall Cavendish International (Asia) Private Limited
A member of Times Publishing Limited
Times Centre, 1 New Industrial Road, Singapore 536196
Tel: (65) 6213 9288   Fax: (65) 6285 4871
E-mail: te@sg.marshallcavendish.com
Online Bookstore: http://www.timesone.com.sg/te

Malaysian Office:
Federal Publications Sdn Berhad (General & Reference Publishing) (3024-D)
Times Subang, Lot 46, Persiaran Teknologi Subang
Subang Hi-Tech Industrial Park
Batu Tiga, 40000 Shah Alam
Selangor Darul Ehsan, Malaysia
Tel: (603) 5635 2191   Fax: (603) 5635 2706
E-mail: cchong@tpg.com.my

National Library Board (Singapore) Cataloguing in Publication Data

Tan, Cecilia.
The family herbal cookbook / Cecilia Tan. — Singapore : Times Editions, 2004.
p. cm.
First published in 1989
ISBN : 981-232-708-8

1. Cookery, Chinese. 2. Cookery (Herbs) I. Title.

TX724.5.C5
641.5951 — dc21   SLS2004021128

Printed in Singapore by Times Graphics (Pte) Ltd

To my husband *See Yin*

and my children

Juliana, Luisa, Dominic and Rachel

CONTENTS

ACKNOWLEDGEMENTS

I would like to express my thanks to the following for the help they have given me in the course of writing this book.

❋ Connie and Alice for typing the many pages;

❋ Brenda, Fadzillah and Faizah for aid rendered;

❋ Annie, Clara, Sook Ying, Soo Hoong, Siew Lan, Christine and Alice for ideas contributed;

❋ my household retainers Hee Moy and Chai Chun for their unfailing patience not only in cooking up the tonics and brews, but also in helping me countercheck facts and fallacies.

Last but not least, I would like to include the many other friends, relatives and herbalists who have helped in one way or another towards making this book a viable one.

FOREWORD

The mere mention of herbs in cooking never fails to provide much food for thought. Herbs, from time immemorial, have been synonymous with health, and the range is vast and complex. The Chinese art of herbal cooking, then, draws upon a long tradition that has been documented for more than 5,000 years and is today practised in the most lowly or lofty of households. In fact, herbs have become so much a part of our daily diet that many of us use them without realising what they are, let alone weigh their efficacy.

Consider, for example, the use of ingredients such as ginger, garlic, onions, soy beans, mint leaves and peppercorns in everyday dishes. It is true that these ingredients and others are used to add variety in taste. More importantly, however, they also have nutritious and curative properties.

In the past, knowledge of the medicinal aspects of herbal cooking were absorbed in the kitchens of mothers and grandmothers. The older generations had the benefit of inheriting tried-and-tested recipes through word of mouth, and also the complex theories that informed those recipes. Thus, their inherent awareness in selecting the right kinds of food for restorative, curative or preventive purposes.

Today, with the decline of the extended family, it has become increasingly difficult to practise and pass on this particular school of cooking. Indeed, a good number of people are losing or have already lost touch with this age-old art. With the contemporary trend towards health foods and healthy eating, it is timely to take a good look once more at this rich heritage of tonic recipes.

The heart of good health is good eating, and herewith a collection of cooking preparations towards this end. Those wary of the esoteric and the exorbitant will appreciate this book since it seeks to inform the reader about the uses of our most natural medicine — foods we eat everyday, foods that graced the tables of our forefathers, foods that nourished them to a ripe old age.

Emerging medical and scientific findings lead some of us to continually rethink our dietary and nutritional habits, and in view of those that have come to light since this book was first published in 1989, tastes have in all likelihood changed. The pursuit of organic foods has since become as pronounced as the rejection of saturated fats and excess salt. In adapting the tradition inherent in herbal cooking to the ongoing health concerns of modern day, the key is in balancing the recognition of the benefits of traditional remedies with a responsible and sensible approach. As such, the use of leaner meat cuts, skinless fowls or organic meats and vegetables are healthier options. So, too, are the sparer use of salt and the replacement of coconut cream with a healthier, albeit less tasty, low-fat alternative if these are your concerns.

INTRODUCTION

Throughout history, the importance of herbs has been acknowledged by people of all nations. The earliest written record of the study of herbs dates back more than 5,000 years when the Sumerians described well-established medicinal uses for such plants as laurel, caraway and thyme.

The ancient Egyptians, as early as 1600 B.C., used elderberry, pomegranate bark, wild lettuce, wormwood, hemlock, garlic, opium, castor oil, coriander, mint, indigo and other herbs for health and as food. The old testament also mentions herb use and cultivation, including mandrake, caraway, wheat, barley and rye.

The brilliant unknown writer (or writers) of the *Hippocratic Collection*, an ancient medical book (circa 300 B.C.), was of the opinion that medicine itself arose with cooks in the kitchen. Since sick people generally do not relish the same kinds of foods they do when they are well, one has to contend that more agreeable, comforting brews were deliberately concocted to soothe, as well as cure their ailing systems. A classic illustration of this can be found in traditional Chinese tonic dishes, which use an awesome pharmacopoeia of Chinese herbs compiled over several thousand years of Chinese civilisation. This established practice is essentially an indigenous product of China's dietary therapy, which uses primarily herbs in special dishes to ward off or cure a variety of illnesses and to strengthen a person's constitution.

Experts in traditional Chinese medicine generally believe that dietary therapy originated as far back as 3,000 B.C., when *Huang Di Nei Jing* or the *Yellow Emperor's Classic of Internal Medicine* was written. This classic, which is also the world's oldest medical textbook, has a list of hundreds of vegetables and fruits and recommends their proper intake based on their observed properties for nutritious and curative purposes. Today, this book is still used by traditional Chinese physicians.

In later dynasties, more medical works on the subject were documented. Hu Sihui, imperial doctor of the Yuan court (A.D. 1271–1368), collected in his three-volume book, *Compendium of Diet*, 94 tonic dish recipes, 35 soup recipes and numerous detailed descriptions of the properties and effects of meat, fruits, tea and spices.

Today, after 5,000 years of study and practice, Chinese traditional herbal therapy recognises over 30,000 herbs and details thousands of recipes for health. Where once these recipes were usually well kept secrets and only the luxuries of members of the imperial families and the rich, today, just about everyone has access to them. Many people enjoy the health benefits of herbs without realising it.

Despite the far-reaching influence of western medicine, this established form of health treatment has not been discarded. On the contrary, the values, properties and use of herbal products are now enjoying a renewed interest as seen in the growing number of Chinese medicinal shops in the newest of shopping centres. The herbalist in each of these shops attract a sizeable number of customers seeking advice and prescriptions for the effective treatment of a whole range of common afflictions, as well as for their general well-being. It is evident, too, from some food outlets and restaurant menus that herbal food preparations are popular choices into the twenty-first century.

For those who prefer to cook, simmer or brew their own herbal concoctions, this book gives a wide range of recipes that meet the nutritional requirements of the young and old. It also introduces the Chinese concept of harmony and balance in food. Apart from herbal brews that supplement the daily diet, there are soups, food dishes and sweets for everyday meals, all of which are delicious and, at the same time, healthy. There are even concoctions that help restore the body's internal balance when its equilibrium is tipped by ailments like coughs, colds and stomach upsets.

How to use this book

It is advisable to go through the introductory sections of this book before using the recipes in it. Here, the Chinese concept of harmony and balance in food is given. A section is devoted to discussing the properties of different ingredients used in herbal cooking, the common and the not-so-common ones. There is also a section on methods of cooking and their merits. The section *Notes on Recipes* gives tips on how to use the recipes to the fullest advantage. There is included in this section, sample menus for making up a balanced meal for the whole family.

The rest of the book is divided into seven sections of recipes, four of them catering to different age groups with their different diet needs. There are also sections for expectant and new mothers and for addressing common ills.

This does not mean that the foods in each section are confined only to the category specified. Foods from the sections *Growing Years* and *Adolescence to Adulthood*, for example, can be prepared for the whole family, while the soups and porridges in the *Babies and Toddlers* section are also good for those with stomach upsets or who are ill.

While food is the natural lifeline of the human body and the right choice of it helps us maintain high levels of vitality and energy, other things — adequate sleep and relaxation of the mind and body — are equally important in helping one achieve a harmonious internal balance of the body to cope with the ups and downs of life.

Last but not least, it is very important to see your doctor for proper medical attention if you are ill. The tonics and brews should only supplement the doctor's medication, especially when the illness is serious.

The Yin/Yang Concept

The Macrocosm

When cooking a Chinese meal, the principle of preparing the correct food in the proper way is of primary importance. Among the many considerations to be taken into account are the choice of ingredients and the requirements of the eater. There has to be harmony and balance in order to ensure that the meal is an equable one for both mind and body.

This sophisticated system of harmonising food is based on the *yin/yang* theory, a concept which pervades Chinese thinking in all areas — everything in the universe is either *yin* or *yang*. This theory recognises that there are two basic and opposing principles that govern the universe and that all phenomena result from their continuous interplay. The twin universal forces, *yin* and *yang*, together form a harmonious whole and one cannot exist without the other. Neither is absolute, and since *yin* and *yang* are always changing, one can become the other according to the rhythm and balance of nature or the universe.

Characteristically, *yin* is represented by femininity, moon, darkness, night, cold, water, earth, autumn and winter, while *yang* is represented by masculinity, sun, heaven, daylight, spring, summer, heat and fire.

The Microcosm

Since the macrocosm is governed by the forces of *yin* and *yang*, man being the microcosm in relation to the universe is also subjected to the same cosmic laws. Hence, certain parts of the body are *yin* while others are *yang*. Diseases that attack the body are the result of an imbalance of *yin* and *yang* in the body. Where harmony is disrupted, and if the *yang* element predominates, there is excitability, anger, hyperactivity and if the *yin* element predominates, there is exhaustion and weakness.

Balance and Harmony in Food

In relation to health, the Chinese concept of eating is also guided by the *yin/ya*ng principle. Since food affects the whole body, the key to healthy eating (as to everything) is a correct balance of *yin* and *yang* at all times. Food is generally classed into three basic categories — **heating** (stimulating to the body), **cooling** (has a calming and sedative effect on the organs) and **neutral** (these are neither stimulating nor sedative and, therefore, can be eaten in reasonable quantities without any undue consequences). The wise person will eat a variety of good, natural and wholesome foods belonging to the category best suited for his or her needs towards achieving harmony and equilibrium within the body.

This philosophy in cooking — a careful attention to balance — is followed by Chinese families when preparing their meals. Some examples are as follows. An excess of sugar or salt is avoided in their meals — the former produces mucus in the nose and throat where it causes catarrh and coughing, while the latter is recognised as a stimulant that affects the kidneys. Sour-tasting foods and liquids are regarded as stimulating to the liver and gall bladder and aid in the secretion of bile so people with weak or categorically cold stomachs should refrain from them. Those already afflicted by a form of impotence should avoid an excess of cooling foods, which may sedate actions of the body's organs too much and affect their rightful functions. Likewise, those suffering from skin infections, rashes, boils, sores and septic spots have to avoid eating foods like beef, crabs, carp, prawns (shrimps) and cherries, which are *yang* foods, or foods that stimulate and generate activity.

Definite claims to the *yin/yang* principle in cooking and its power to cure all illnesses in the body will continue to be a debatable issue. For some, myself included, aligning with the concept leads to a greater harmonisation of the *yin* and *yang* within our bodies, failing which our bodies would never come close to a happy and healthy state. Our diets, then, should as far as possible be correctly balanced at all times.

Methods of Cooking

Boiling

This method of cooking is commonly employed when preparing herbal soups or to give a soft texture to the foods cooked. In this type of cooking, the liquid in which the food is cooked boils, and not the food itself. Foods typically cooked in boiling liquid include vegetables, meats and eggs. When the liquid boils, reduce the temperature so that the liquid just bubbles.

Simmering or slow cooking

This is a slow form of boiling. The temperature is usually not too high and the duration of cooking this way can last from one to three hours. When foods are simmered in liquid, there is just an occasional bubble or two on the surface. Stews, soups and sauces are simmered to bring out the flavour or aroma of the preparation. This is also the favoured method when cooking to thicken a mixture and to bring out a complex variety of flavours. In the case of the latter, the dish is cooked for several hours until the liquid is reduced by a quarter or half.

Simmering or slow cooking goes very well with the use of charcoal fire. Indeed, the older generation maintains that nothing beats the aroma and taste of cooking in a clay pot over a charcoal stove. For those with no time or desire to fan coal, a gas burner or a slow cooker is just as good, and cleaner to boot. Since gentle heat diffused throughout a pot is the prime requirement for any long cooking, simmering is usually done in pots (refer to *Cooking Utensils*) that are best suited to several hours of slow cooking without boiling over.

Frying

This is a quick and convenient method of cooking foods in fat. It gives an excellent crisp and golden texture to the foods. There are four ways of frying. The utensil most suited is a wok because its special shape allows for the use of less oil than normal and its thin metal facilitates quicker, more precise temperature control.

Deep-frying involves total or near total immersion of the food in hot oil. It is used not only to crisp batter-coated morsels, but also to cook marinated foods (fish and spare ribs) or precook food which is served with a sauce.

To test the oil for deep-frying, drop a cube of bread into the pan. If it sinks, the oil is not hot enough. If it frizzles gently, it is right for medium-fast frying. If it turns golden in one minute, it is suitable for fast frying.

Do not fry too much at once or the fat will cool. The fried items, when cooked, should be removed and drained on a piece of absorbent kitchen paper. The amount of oil used depends entirely on the size of the food pieces to be immersed. When cooking a whole chicken or fish, the oil should only half immerse it. The exposed part should be cooked by spooning oil over it for half the cooking time before turning it and repeating the process.

Shallow-frying is sometimes used as an alternative to deep-frying. Here, much less oil (about four to six tablespoons) than in deep-frying is used. The temperature is also regulated to moderately hot. After cooking, the fried items should be drained on a wire rack or on a piece of absorbent kitchen paper.

Dry-frying is for foods with plenty of natural fat and so no coating is required. Some types of beans, eg black beans, are also dry-fried or toasted before being cooked in soups.

Stir-frying involves the very rapid cooking of small pieces of food or vegetables in very little oil. Since stir-frying requires minimal time, meats, fish and vegetables are cut into small pieces. Stir-frying is the most commonly practised form of Asian cooking. From the health point of view, cooking this way preserves the original flavour and texture of the food, and its nutrients. The food also retains its crunch, freshness and crispness.

To stir-fry vegetables, put a few tablespoons of oil in a wok. When the oil is hot, add in the vegetables and use a long-handled ladle to toss and stir fast in order to seal in the juices and keep the ingredients fresh. Dish out and serve immediately while still hot. As the vegetables cool, their juices will escape. They will also turn yellow and become overcooked.

Steaming

This is a gentle method of cooking by intense, concentrated moist heat, ie steam. It is a popular way of cooking minced meat, vegetables and seafood. It is also the best way to cook whole fish without the fear of breaking the skin and flesh.

Again, the wok can be used for efficient steaming if you do not have a steamer. Add water to the wok and bring to the boil. Position a rack or other perforated surface, eg a metal colander, over the boiling water, then place food that has been arranged on a dish or in a bowl on top. Cover the wok and let the food cook. If the wok is drying out, replenish by pouring boiling hot water down the side of the wok.

Another method is to fill a porcelain or heatproof (flameproof) bowl with the ingredients, and then place the bowl in a large pot of boiling water. Cover the pot and steam as required.

Steamed food, especially fish dishes, should be removed when cooked and served at once. Avoid reheating steamed food as it changes the texture of the food.

Pressure cooking

Pressure cooking is a method of cooking food in steam but differs from the normal method of steaming because none of the steam escapes. Instead, the steam is forced to reach extremely high temperatures and when trapped, works to cut cooking time by as much as 75 per cent.

Recipes in this book that call for simmering can sometimes also be pressure cooked. In those cases, reduce cooking time by one-third or up to half.

Double-boiling

This method of cooking is believed to seal in nutrients and flavour in a manner that cannot be equalled by other methods of cooking. Double-boiling is usually done over charcoal heat and cooking time generally extends to four hours. Less than that gives too little time for the flavours to seal in, while more than that destroys the nutrients.

Double-boiling differs from steaming in that steam is not applied directly to the food to cook it. Rather, steam is used to heat a closed container holding the food, hence the long period of time needed.

Cooking Utensils for Herbal Cooking

Clay pots

Clay-pot cooking is synonymous with slow charcoal burning, which is reputed to bring out the flavour and nutrients better than stove top heat fuelled by gas or electricity. It is an ancient method much favoured in China and was especially invaluable during the winter season as these earthen pots retained heat well.

Clay pots come in many shapes and sizes. Some have spouts to facilitate pouring, while others as large as stock pots are fortified with wire mesh.

Unglazed clay pots were traditionally used for herbal and medicinal brews. They need gentle handling because they crack easily with heat. To prevent cracking during cooking, soak the pots in cold water for about 20 minutes, then drain before use.

To season a new unglazed clay pot, fill the pot with used grated coconut and leave it over dying embers atop a charcoal stove. Repeat the process a few times. Alternatively, pour boiling water into the clay pot and leave to stand for 48 hours.

Unglazed clay pots are very porous and will absorb the smell of detergent used in washing up. It is best to clean these pots by filling with hot water and then leaving to stand for 30 minutes.

Glazed clay pots require equally delicate handling but can be washed with liquid detergent in some warm water because their surfaces have been sealed. If there are stubborn stains, soak in hot water before rubbing briskly.

Double-boilers

Double-boiling is traditionally done with a set of two pots, one slightly smaller than the other. The smaller pot is placed inside the bigger pot, but rests suspended near the rim. Food is placed in the smaller, inner container, and water in the larger.

With heat, water boils and bubbles in the larger container and steam rises to heat the smaller, suspended container and cook the food inside. As very little evaporation occurs in this form of cooking, use only required amounts of liquid and not more.

Instead of the two-pot double-boiler, some people prefer to use a porcelain device the Cantonese call *dun chung*, a container with two lids; one flat and the other dome-shaped. To use, place this container, with both lids secured, into a pot of boiling water and then cover the pot. Care should be taken with the water level so that the water, when boiling, does not splash over the container.

Enamel-coated cookware

The better grade ones are of heavy metals such as cast-iron and reinforced aluminium. Care has to be taken that the enamel inside is not chipped as rusting can occur. Enamel ware can be used in place of metal pots, especially when cooking acidic food, but ensure that these have top quality coating.

Slow cookers

Made famous by the brand *Crock Pot*, this is a heavy, glazed earthen pot that comes with an outer metal pot fitted with an electrically heated element and a heavy glass cover. It looks much like a rice cooker and essentially works on the same principles.

The slow cooker is the modern answer to long simmering and there is rarely any burning or charring. Unlike using clay pots, there is also no need to add water from time to time during the cooking process as very little evaporation takes place. It also eliminates the possibility of boiling over. When using a slow cooker, halve the amount of liquid required in normal simmering.

Steamers

Traditionally, Chinese steaming baskets made from bamboo are used. These are stacked one on top of the other and placed in a wok or specially built boiler filled with boiling water. The level of water does not reach the base of the lowest steaming basket. A lid covers the top basket. Steam rising from the water forces its way through all the baskets to the top, cooking all the dishes simultaneously.

Dishes that require the least cooking are put in the upper baskets, and those that require the most cooking in the lower baskets. If cooking only one dish, use only one steaming basket and the lid.

There is a special steamer for herbal cooking that is made of clay and has a funnel in the middle that allows steam to enter the cavity of the container, which is covered by a lid. This container is placed on a steaming rack in a pot of boiling water. The steam from the boiling water enters the funnel's opening at the bottom of the container to cook the food inside.

Pressure cookers

This is a time-saving cooking utensil ideal for cooking meats and ingredients that need long cooking to tenderise and bring out the flavour. When using a pressure cooker, never fill more than two-thirds the pot's capacity or food particles will later block the valve. After use, wash immediately in warm water. Wash the lid, rubber ring and clean the valve channel under a jet of running water.

Remove any particles which could clog the vent pipe by wiping. Also, make sure the safety valve is correctly set. If food is stuck to the base, soak in cold water for several hours to loosen. Store the cooker open or it may take on a musty smell.

Ensure that the rubber seal around the lid, also known as a gasket, is in good condition as once it loses its flexibility, steam will escape and the cooker will not be so effective. Replace the rubber ring at least once every two years.

Unglazed clay pot

Glazed clay pot

Slow cooker

Double-boiler

Funnel steamer

Dun chung

Enamel-coated cookware

Bamboo steamer

Notes on Recipes

Weights, measures and proportions

Your neighbourhood herbalist or *sinseh* is the acknowledged expert when it comes to weighing and combining the right proportion of each type of herb, root, bark or seed for a specific dish. He or she usually does this based on the number of people eating and the amounts of accompanying ingredients used. Since most herbs are dried and light in nature, the weights and amounts indicated are guidelines. In the final analysis, the proportion of each ingredient used depends on individual taste. You can, after familiarising yourself with the more common ingredients (note: not the more potent herbs), experiment with your own combinations. Those with a liking for clear soup, for example, could stick to the minimum of herbs and ingredients, while those who prefer hearty blends of rich gravies can increase the ingredients that combine to give the desired multifaceted flavour and taste.

For those who have little to no idea about herbal cooking, it would be best to rely on the herbalist to portion the ingredients, adjusting blends and proportions to taste only at a later stage. It would be wise to bear in mind that in certain recipes, ingredients must be properly matched and balanced or else the dishes could smell peculiar or lose their desired curative effects. While more rock sugar or dried longan added to a brew to pander to a sweet tooth in no way upsets the equilibrium of a dish, increasing the amount of potent herbs like ginseng or Chinese angelica (*dang gui / dong kwai*) beyond what is stipulated in a recipe unduly tips the scales and renders the dish into something other than what was intended.

Liquid measurements

Flexibility can be exercised to a great degree when using liquid measures in brewing herbs (bearing in mind also the constitution of the person for whom the dish is being prepared). Some like their brews hearty and thick, while others may have to subscribe to lighter brews because they have sensitive digestive systems. Ultimately, the desired thickness or concentration depends very much (as in anything to do with food) on individual tastes, which vary considerably.

If a recipe calls for simmering until liquid is reduced by half, it is meant for cooking over a gas or charcoal stove. When using a slow cooker, use half the stated quantity of liquid as little to no evaporation takes place.

On the other hand, where the finished dish has to retain the same amount of liquid as that used, one needs to top up when cooking over a gas or charcoal stove. This is unnecessary in the case of cooking in a slow cooker.

In this book, liquid measurements are also given in bowl measurements, that is, the Chinese rice bowl. This makes it that much easier since soups, stews and tonics are usually served in bowls.

Getting your money's worth

The brew: The less fastidious who believe in getting their money's worth from tonic brews do not have to immediately discard the sediment after the derived liquid is drunk. As in the case of squeezing out a second coconut milk, a thinner brew can also be obtained by adding a bowl or two of hot water and simmering the herbal concoction a second time. Obviously, the resultant brew will be much less aromatic in taste and smell.

The meat: Meats that are used in tonic brews are usually considered tasteless after hours of slow simmering or steaming. Hence, many people do not eat them after downing the derived liquid. In the old days, however, many mothers would drink the brew and give their children the meats. Apart from not wasting food, this was because brews of strong concoctions such as stewed chicken and ginseng are not suitable for young bodies, being too potent and overpowering, whereas the meat is all right for them to consume. So if your children do not mind boiled meats, serve to them with a drip or two of soy sauce.

Go it slow

Do not go on a sudden binge of herbal brews or food preparations using lots of herbs. It will cause an upheaval in your body's system. Although any Chinese herbalist will vouch that taking Chinese herbs regularly will build up your body's defences against disease and restore your health, taking potent herbal tonics day in and week out is likely to wreak havoc and create an imbalance instead.

Those with serious ailments such as kidney problems should check with their doctors first before trying out the more potent recipes. People who suffer from high blood pressure and any form of heart ailment are advised to stay clear of potent herbal brews.

Choice of cooking methods and meats

Cooking methods: This has to be a personal decision. You have to weigh your personal preferences and beliefs against the pros and cons of certain cooking methods — double-boiling, slow cooking or pressure cooking. Tradition dies hard for many from the old school who still believe that nutrition is diminished and valuable meat juices are lost in forms of cooking other than double-boiling.

Choice of meats: The fresher and leaner the cut, the better, obviously. When a recipe calls for chicken, traditionalists will never use battery chickens. For them, only free range chickens will do. One might ask what is the fuss about. Just imagine the artificial hormonal inputs in a chicken slowly being leached out during the three to four hours of slow cooking, and those inputs later going into your system.

Boiled water

Where a recipe calls for liquid to be used, especially water, this has to be boiled first. Tap water or unboiled water should not be used in herbal cooking. It is true that hot, boiling water shortens cooking time but more importantly, boiled water is also cleaned of any unhealthy properties during the boiling process.

24-hour abstinence

If you do not already know, it is standard practice to refrain from taking Chinese radish in any form within 24 hours of imbibing a herbal or tonic brew. Chinese radish has such strong cleansing properties that it will destroy all curative and nutritive elements in dishes that one consumes in the same meal with it. In the old days, staunch believers of this practice would abstain from radish for three days to a month after consuming a herbal brew. Other foods to abstain from are acidic or sharp fruit, such as pineapples and oranges.

Cross referencing

The notes accompanying certain recipes should be cross referenced with the section on ingredients. In fact, a run through this section will give you a clearer idea of the curative nature of certain recipes.

While the recipes have been grouped according to age groups for easier reference (eg in *Motherhood*, recipes for confinement can be found), there are numerous recipes that are relevant to more than one age group. Sweet herbal brews, for instance, are understandably liked by both young and old, and good for all age groups too. Likewise, certain herbal tonics that are strengthening, recuperative and beneficial to the ailing are also good for those with a weak constitution. Broths which are grouped under *Babies and Toddlers* also can be prescribed for the sensitive stomachs of the sick as they are easily digested. Notes on individual recipes indicate whether they are good for age groups other than the one they fall under.

Vacuum flask plus

The vacuum flask is an indispensable storage item for tonics and brews that are to be consumed before going to bed. It is a time-saving and convenient answer to having to heat up tonics and brews before bedtime. Before using the vacuum flask, rinse with very hot water. Soups can also stay hot enough if a meal is delayed for hours.

Serving per recipe

Recipes are for four to six persons, except for those in *Babies and Toddlers*, *Motherhood* and *Aids for Common Ills* which are for two persons at the most. Recipes in these three sections are not generally recommended for the whole family and do not always appeal to everyone, hence the smaller proportions.

Sample menus

For a family of six persons consisting of two grandparents, parents and two children; one adolescent and one under 12:

Main meal:
- ✻ Rice
- ✻ Chicken feet and black bean soup (*The Fifties and Beyond*)
- ✻ Stir-fried health platter (*Adolescence to Adulthood*)
- ✻ Scallops and bean curd (*The Growing Years — Twelve Years and Under*)
- ✻ Double-boiled eggs with minced pork (*Babies and Toddlers*)

Dessert:
- ✻ Red bean porridge (*Adolescence to Adulthood*)

Since there are elderly persons (grandparents), the menu cannot include dishes that are either too rich or oily. Chicken feet and black bean soup is nutritious, fortifying and light enough for every family member. The rest of the dishes are varied and tasty to cater to the younger members of the family. On the whole, the menu is substantial and healthy without being too heavy. The balance is achieved through a combination of soup, vegetables and meat. A sweet dessert rounds up this meal.

For a family of four persons consisting of parents and two children:

Main meal:
- ✻ Rice
- ✻ Stir-fried anchovies with celery (*Adolescence to Adulthood*)
- ✻ Stir-fried spinach (*The Growing Years — Twelve Years and Under*)
- ✻ Trotter with Chinese radish and ginger (*Adolescence to Adulthood*)

Dessert:
- ✻ Red bean porridge (*Adolescence to Adulthood*)

There are fewer dishes in this menu because there are fewer persons and the trotter is a heavy dish. To balance this slightly oily and wholesome dish are two stir-fried vegetable dishes for variety and crunch.

Ingredients Used in Herbal Cooking

The associative connotation of herbs as bitter-tasting ingredients for use in the preparation of tonics and brews is such that we often lose sight of the fact that common ingredients such as garlic, onion, watercress and carrot have been used for their medicinal properties since time immemorial. Likewise, to this day, taken-for-granted edibles like barley and celery play a part in contemporary folk medicine as herbal ingredients.

Below is a table of main ingredients showing their common names in English, phonetically spelt Cantonese and Mandarin characters, as well as whether they are cooling, heating or neutral in energy.

English	Cantonese	Chinese Characters	Property
abalone (canned)	bau yue	鲍鱼	neutral
abalone (dried)	so bau	苏鲍	neutral
agar-agar (Japanese gelatin)	tai choy goh	燕菜	cooling
amaranth (Chinese spinach)	yeen choy	苋菜	cooling
anchovy	kong yue chai	江鱼仔	heating
angelica root, Chinese	dong kwai	当归	heating
astragalus root	puk kei	黄芪	heating
barley	yi mai	薏米	cooling
beans:			
adzuki bean	chek siew dau	赤小豆	neutral
black bean	hak dau	黑豆	neutral
black-eyed bean	mei dau	眉豆	neutral
broad bean	chan dau	蚕豆	neutral
hyacinth bean	been dau	扁豆	neutral
kidney bean	yew dau	腰豆	neutral
mung (green) bean	lok dau	绿豆	cooling
red adzuki bean	hung dau	红豆	neutral
soy bean	wong dau	黄豆	cooling
bean sprout	dau ngah	豆芽	cooling
beef	ngau yok	牛肉	heating
bird's nest	yeen wor	燕窝	neutral
black chicken	chok si gai	竹丝鸡	heating
black glutinous rice	hak nor mai	黑糯米	neutral
black vinegar, Chinese	hak cho	黑醋	cooling

boxthorn fruit (Chinese wolfberry)	gei chi	枸杞子	cooling
boxthorn leaf	gau gei choy	枸杞菜	cooling
Buddha's fruit	lor hawn gor	罗汉果	cooling
carrot	hung lor bak	红萝卜	heating
celery, Chinese	kun choy	芹菜	cooling
chicken	gai	鸡	heating
chive, Chinese	gau choy	韭菜	heating
chrysanthemum	gok fa	菊花	cooling
cnidium root	chuen kung	川芎	heating
codonopsis root	dong sum	党参	heating
cogongrass root	maw gun	白茅根	cooling
cooking wine, Chinese	fa dew	花雕酒	heating
cordyceps	tung chung cho	冬虫夏草	heating
crab	hai	蟹	cooling
cuttlefish	yau yue	鱿鱼	neutral
dates:			
black date	hak cho	黑枣	heating
red date	hung cho	红枣	heating
southern date	nam cho	南枣	heating
sweet date	mut cho	蜜枣	heating
donkey's glue	ah kau	阿胶	heating
dried oyster	ho see	蚝干	neutral
dried scallop	kong yue chee	干贝	neutral
eggs:			
chicken	gai dan	鸡蛋	heating
quail	um chun dan	鹌鹑蛋	heating
salted (duck)	ham dan	咸蛋	cooling
fish:			
catfish	tong sut yue	塘虱鱼	neutral
marble goby (ikan hantu)	sang yue	生鱼	cooling
pomfret (white)	bak chong yue	白鲳鱼	cooling
threadfin	mah yau yue	马幼鱼	cooling
French bean	gwai dau	季豆	neutral

frog's leg	teen gai	田鸡	heating
fungus:			
black (wood ear) fungus	mok yi	黑木耳	neutral
cloud ear fungus	wun yi	云耳	neutral
white (silver) fungus	shuet yi	白木耳	heating
garlic	shuen tau	蒜头	heating
ginger	keong	姜	heating
gingko nut	bak gor	白果	cooling
ginseng:			
American	yong sum	花旗参	heating
Chinese	yan sum	人参	heating
Korean	go lai sum	高丽参	heating
glutinous rice	nor mai	糯米	neutral
hasima	shuet kup	雪蛤	cooling
kudzu shoot	got choy	葛菜	neutral
lamb	yeong yok	羊肉	heating
lily bud (golden needle)	kum chum	金针菜	cooling
lily bulb petal	bak hup	百合	neutral
longan	lung ngan	龙眼	heating
lotus root	leen ngau	莲藕	cooling
lotus seed	leen chi	莲子	cooling
marrow	lo wong kwa	老黄瓜	cooling
milk	ngau lai	牛奶	neutral
mint leaf	bok hor yip	薄荷叶	cooling
mushroom, Chinese	tung gu	冬菇	neutral
mustard cabbage	gai choy	芥菜	cooling
noodles:			
egg noodles	meen	鸡蛋面	heating
rice vermicelli	mai fun	米粉	neutral
fine rice vermicelli	meen seen	面线	neutral
transparent vermicelli	fun see	粉丝	neutral
onion	dai chung tau	洋葱	heating
palm sugar (gula melaka)	yeh tong	椰糖	heating
peanut (groundnut)	fa sung	花生	neutral
pigeon	bak kup	鸽子	neutral
pig's kidney	juih yew	猪腰	neutral

pig's liver	juih yurn	猪肝	neutral
pig's stomach	juih toh	猪肚	neutral
pork	juih yok	猪肉	heating
potato	hor lan she	马铃薯	neutral
pepper (ground)	wu chiu fun	胡椒粉	heating
peppercorn	wu chiu lup	胡椒粒	heating
radish, Chinese	lor bak	白萝卜	cooling
rice wine	mai chow	米酒	heating
screwpine (pandan) leaf	um peh yip	班兰叶	cooling
sea cucumber	hoi sum	海参	cooling
sesame seed	chi ma	芝麻	heating
sesame seed oil	ma yao	麻油	heating
shark's fin	yue chee	鱼翅	neutral
shallot	chung tau chai	小葱头	heating
snow pea	hor lan dau	荷兰豆	neutral
Solomon's seal	yok chok	玉竹	neutral
soy beans:			
bean curd, soft	dau fu	豆腐	cooling
bean curd, hard	dau gon	豆干	neutral
red fermented bean curd	nam yue	南乳	cooling
dried bean curd stick	fu chok	腐竹	neutral
soybean paste	dau cheong	豆瓣酱	cooling
spring onion	chung	葱	heating
sugar cane	chok cheh	竹蔗	cooling
sweet potato	fan she	番薯	neutral
tomato	fan kare	番茄	cooling
turmeric	wong keong	黄姜	cooling
water chestnut	ma thai	马蹄	cooling
watercress	sai yong choy	西洋菜	cooling
watermelon	sai kwa	西瓜	cooling
white atractylodes	bak surt	白术	neutral
winter melon	tung kwa	冬瓜	cooling
winter melon strip (sugared)	tung kwa tong	冬瓜糖	cooling
yam (taro)	woo tau	芋头	neutral
yam, Chinese	wai san	山药	neutral

Glossary of Ingredients

Abalone

This is a smooth-textured mollusc. The meat is firm and chewy in consistency. Into the twenty-first century, Australia and Japan are the world's leading exporters of abalone, usually sold canned or dried. Abalone is said to be good for relieving stress and burnout when cooked as a tonic. Here, only the dried form can be used.

Canned abalone is more convenient to use than its dried counterpart, which needs many hours of boiling to render it tender enough to eat. Food connoiseurs, however, regard dried abalone as far superior to tinned ones. Both types are pricey, nevertheless.

Adzuki bean (*chi xiao dou* / *chek siew dau*)

A relative of the more famous red adzuki bean (*hong dou* / *hung dau*), the adzuki bean is darker in colour and is further distinguished by a black line along the centre of its white seed scar. These beans aid in relieving rheumatism, strengthening weak legs, and clearing wind and gas from the stomach. To use, first wash well under running water in a colander and drain.

Agar-agar

Also known as Japanese gelatin, agar-agar is a clear, glutinous seaweed sold in strips. It is used instead of gelatin for sweets and because it sets without refrigeration, it is suited to hot climates. Seaweed contains iodine, vitamins A, B and E, and traces of magnesium, copper, silver, titanium, nickel, chromium, barium, sulphur, sodium and many other minerals. It prevents goitre, relieves congestion, breaks up phlegm and reduces fever. To use, soak in cold water for 5 to 10 minutes, then cook as directed.

Amaranth (*xian cai* / *yeen choy*)

Also known as Chinese spinach, this green, leafy vegetable is high in iron and contains vitamins A and C. Whether raw or semi-cooked, amaranth is a detoxifying agent for bodies suffering from alcohol poisoning. Not to be confused with spinach (*bo cai* / *bor choy*), which has hollow stems, the stems of amaranth are solid.

Anchovy (*jiang yu zai* / *kong yue chai*)

In its cured form (dried and salted), this small fish, known as *ikan bilis* in Malay, is indispensably popular with cooks, especially for making soup stock. Although anchovy cubes are readily available in the shops, nothing beats preparing the stock yourself.

Anchovies are used liberally in making soup stocks for children because of their high calcium content. Rare would be the mother who does not anchor her children's diet with this well-loved little fish.

To use, first remove the heads and backbones, then soak in water for a few minutes before draining well and leaving to dry in the sun for at least one hour.

Angelica root, Chinese (*dang gui* / *dong kwai*)

Highly prized and sought after for the treatment of a host of women's ills or ailments related to the female constitution, Chinese angelica is said to build blood, nourish the female organs, regulate menstruation and alleviate period pains, relieve menopausal discomforts such as hot flushes and counter general weakness and lethargy. Chinese angelica also has fatty components that, when cooked, become beneficial for diabetic patients.

Herbal shops generally sell Chinese angelica as dried but unprocessed pieces of root. Some shops sell Chinese angelica that has been processed into capsules. In its dried state, Chinese angelica emits a certain woody aroma that develops into a strong, pungent flavour when cooked. It is usually steamed or simmered with a combination of chicken, mutton or pork and other herbs, depending on the nature of the ailment to be addressed. The root requires no preparation before cooking.

Herbalists often advise those taking Chinese angelica to avoid consuming strong root teas, eg ginseng tea, or fruit, especially the cooling variety, soon after or before. This is so as to reap the optimum health benefits of the Chinese angelica.

Astragalus root (*huang qi* / *puk kei*)

The root is yellowish-brown in colour, with a mild taste not unlike licorice. Research has revealed that astragalus root is effective in checking diabetes and perspiration that results from tuberculosis. The herb is a favourite remedy for feelings of general weakness and nervous exhaustion. Mood swings and emotional upsets can also be reduced with this aromatic wonder. For this reason, active adolescents who expend a lot of energy and adults who are subjected to the pressures of life could do with the root's curative properties. The root's effectiveness in promoting blood circulation is also legendary. In so doing, it helps vasodilation and reduces blood pressure. Because of its manifold benefits for a wide range of ills, astragalus root is widely used in everyday stews or soups as an aid to good health.

Barley

When pearl barley, or barley that has been hulled, is cooked, a mucilaginous substance is obtained and that substance is a good source of nutrition for those with sore throats or weak stomachs. As it is easily digested, barley is a non-irritating food ideal for those suffering from inflammatory conditions of the bowels or of the mucous membranes of the body. Barley, as such, is good for children suffering from diarrhoea. Barley can also whet the appetites of the sick and convalescent. Barley water is often given to babies or children suffering from fever. Many Chinese households also prepare barley water on hot days in a bid to cool heated bodies or constitutions.

Beans

Alongside cereals, beans are an important food for humankind. Some varieties, in fact, have a protein content higher than any other vegetable and can act as a substitute for animal protein. Beans are also rich in vitamin B, minerals and carbohydrates and are used in an enormous variety of dishes, including soups, desserts and porridges. The possibilities are as numerous as your imagination allows.

The variety of beans most commonly used for cooking includes soy beans, adzuki beans, mung (green) beans, black beans, kidney beans and broad beans. Today, beans are a basic food in parts of the world where animal protein and food in general is scarce. Since beans take longer than other foods to digest, they help to keep hunger at bay for that much longer.

Do not cook beans over high heat or too quickly as their skins will break as a result. Simmering them over low heat also helps make the dish more flavourful. Salt acts to toughen beans and consequently slows their cooking. Acids such as those in wine, vinegar and lemon juice also slow down their softening process, so add these condiments only when the beans are almost cooked.

Beef

Beef is the most nourishing of all red meat and good quality beef is easily digestible. Since beef is a 'heaty' food, an excessive intake of the meat not only causes the body to overheat, but can also leads to intestinal disorders, so avoid overindulging in this meat. Some people are allergic to beef and have reported developing skin irritations such as boils, sores, itches and rashes after eating the meat.

Bird's nest (*yan wo* / *yeen wor*)

Sea swallows or swifts produce a gelatinous substance to coat their nests and it is this gelatinous part of the nest that the Chinese have traditionally regarded as both delicacy and tonic food. Aside from promising general good health, bird's nest is also believed to specifically ward off influenza and the common cold.

Because such nests are usually perched on cliffs, obtaining them is a difficult and often life-threatening task, resulting in the considerable prices of bird's nest in the shops. Apart from China, Borneo and parts of Indochina are also known to produce bird's nest. Sold by weight in herbal shops, bird's nest is available in three forms — whole cups, broken cups or chips, and loose fragments. You can buy them cleaned or uncleaned, with the latter requiring long, tedious and careful preparation.

With cleaned bird's nest, soak in cold water for two hours before cooking, separate the pieces if necessary and drain before adding to the pot. With uncleaned bird's nest, soak in water for two days so that the embedded feathers and tiny twigs can be more easily removed. Once cleaned of impurities, wash and drain before cooking.

Black (wood ear) fungus (*hei mu er / mok yi*)

Dark brown to black in colour, black fungus, also known as wood ear fungus, is thicker and crunchier than the similar-looking cloud ear fungus (*yun er / wun yi*). Wood ear fungus is reputed to be good for clearing blood clots and cleansing the womb, which is why it is frequently used in meals for women observing the after-birth confinement period. It can be bought from supermarkets or provision shops. Prepare as you would cloud ear fungus.

Black vinegar, Chinese (*hei cu / hak cho*)

Many Chinese dishes include black vinegar, which is traditionally made from glutinous rice and has a relatively pungent flavour. Vinegar, however, leaches the goodness from food, including calcium from the bones that are cooked with it. If unavailable, substitute with malt or white Chinese vinegar (*bai cu / bak cho*).

Boxthorn fruit (*gou qi zi / gei chi*)

Also known as the Chinese wolfberry, boxthorn fruit is small, bright red, fleshy and sweet to the taste. The fruit possesses numerous healing properties and is known to help correct poor eyesight resulting from malnutrition, heal the diabetic, restore the strength of the sick and activate kidney and liver functions. It is especially effective in addressing eye diseases such as vessel expansion and inflammation.

From ancient times, boxthorn fruit has been used by the Chinese in conjunction with other herbs, especially Chinese yam (*shan yao / wai san*), to create remedies for worn-out tissues and to pep up energy. To this day, growing children and working adults are often prescribed brews of this berry to relieve eyestrain (from watching too much television or working too long in front of the computer) and increase their energy.

Buddha's fruit (*luo han guo / lor hawn gor*)

Buddha's fruit is sold in its dried form and has a brittle, brownish-green shell. Favoured for its slightly cooling properties, Buddha's fruit is used mostly in sweet brews to alleviate conditions such as ulcers, boils and an overheated body.

To use, wipe the outer shell with a clean, wet cloth, then break into halves or smaller pieces and cook as directed.

Carrot

Carrots are an excellent source of carotene and vitamin A, both of which contribute to good vision, especially night vision. Hot carrot soup is a perennial favourite of caring mothers who use it in a bid to cool body heat and to combat a number of ills. As it is easily digestible, the soup is also an effective remedy for those suffering from stomach and intestinal upsets, including diarrhoea. Eating raw carrots can rid the body of roundworms because they contain a relevant essential oil, while drinking fresh carrot juice can relieve stomach acidity, congestion in the chest and heartburn. Aside from these detoxifying attributes, the high potassium salt content in carrots also make them an excellent diuretic.

Carrot is a versatile ingredient to cook. It combines well with other foods and also adds a certain sweetness to the dish because of the large amount of sugar it contains. Avoid scraping or peeling carrots where possible as the flavour lies mostly in the skin or just under it. Caution should be exercised, however, when using old carrots or those sold in polythene bags as some may have developed a dead and slushy layer on the surface that will have to be scraped. Buy fresh, unwashed carrots as far as possible.

Chicken
A highly nutritious bird, chicken is held in high esteem by the Chinese, so much so that it is an integral part of festive fare during auspicious occasions. As far as possible, choose free range chickens over battery hens for tonic purposes. Although they are a little more pricey, free range chickens are free of artificial hormones and less fatty. Chicken carcass is the skeleton of the chicken after the flesh has been removed. It is usually used for making chicken stock.

Chinese celery (*qin cai* / *kun choy*)
Chinese celery contains vitamins A, B and C, lots of calcium, potassium, phosphorus, sodium and iron and smaller amounts of sulphur, silicon and magnesium.

The herb is highly recommended for arthritis, lumbago, neuralgia and nervousness. It is also said to alleviate hypertension, mild diabetes, insomnia, coughs, headaches, flatulence and poor appetite, as well as regulate kidney functions by inducing an increased flow of urine. People with chronic kidney problems, however, should moderate their intake, as should pregnant women because Chinese celery promotes the onset of menstruation.

Consumed raw in a salad or in the form of freshly made juice, Chinese celery can help clear up skin problems. Hot tea made from the seeds is known for neutralising uric acids and other excess acids in the body.

Chinese cooking wine (*hua tiao* / *fa dew*)
In Chinese cooking, cooking wine more often than not refers to *hua tiao* wine, in particular that originating from the region Shao Xing in China. Because the region came to earn a reputation over time for producing quality *hua tiao* wine, the pale, clear wine is sometimes also referred to as *shao xing* wine.

If unavailable, use a pale, dry sherry and halve the amount specified in the recipe. Like Chinese rice wines, *hua tiao* is used for its warming properties.

Chinese mushrooms

Dried Chinese mushrooms are commonly included in herbal cooking where meats are used. They impart a delightful smoky aroma and a definitive flavour, even if using only a few. Mushrooms are a source of minerals. They are filling and not fattening but can absorb a large quantity of fat or oil in the process of cooking. Any weight of dried mushrooms equals five times that weight in fresh mushrooms. Before use, soak mushrooms in water for 15 to 20 minutes. Save the liquid for cooking.

Chinese radish (*luo bo* / *lor bak*)

This cooling root vegetable is excellent as an antidote for combating slight cases of poisoning. In fact, a tablespoon or two of fresh radish juice will have near-immediate remedial effect in relieving a congested stomach due to overindulgence in strong herbs or indigestion from overly rich foods. This potent cleansing action of Chinese radish is also such that those taking herbs or other nourishing or medicinal brews are usually advised to abstain from eating it for a day or two afterwards to prevent all the nutrients in the prescription from being destroyed.

Chinese yam (*shan yao* / *wai san*)

Extolled for its wide-ranging health benefits, Chinese yam has a fairly modest appearance — chalk-white slivers. Chinese yam has been recorded as having the ability to enhance vigour, promote muscle growth and repair worn-out tissue, facilitate gonadal functions and alleviate bodily weakness after long-term illness.

The herb has also been said to effectively counter diabetes, diarrhoea, kidney defects, coughing and dehydration. It can, however, cause frequent urination and perspiration. Chinese yam is usually used in conjunction with meats and other herbs to aid digestion, regulate the body's sugar level and control inflammation of the uterus.

Chrysanthemum (*ju hua* / *gok fa*)

Dried chrysanthemum flowers are popularly used to make tea, which is famous for having a cooling effect on fevers or overheating bodies, as well as a soothing effect on headaches. Chrysanthemum also has a reputation for improving weak eyesight and bad circulation, subduing pains, soothing inflammation and infections and relieving digestive upsets, especially those arising from eating overly rich foods.

Cloud ear fungus (*yun er* / *wun yi*)

Cloud ear fungus comes in dried pieces measuring about 3 cm in diameter. Ranging from dark brown to black in colour, the crinkly pieces gain a gelatinous texture after cooking. To use, first soak in hot water for 20 to 25 minutes, then rinse well, drain and snip into smaller pieces if desired.

Cnidium root (*chuan xiong / chuen kung*)

Known to alleviate headaches, cnidium root usually takes the form of thin slices at herbal shops. Irregularly shaped and brown in colour, the slices do not need any preparation before use.

Codonopsis root (*dang shen / dong sum*)

Codonopsis root has many tonic uses. It promotes salivation and aid digestion, relieves diarrhoea and severe coughing, reduces nausea and weakness after severe bleeding, activates metabolism and improves blood circulation, alleviates diabetes, stabilises nervousness and counters extreme mental and physical fatigue.

   The root is usually cooked with meats in soups and stews to promote general good health. To use, cut pieces of the root into 3-cm lengths if they are too long and add to the pot. Do not wash.

Cordyceps (*dong chong xia cao / tung chung cho*)

A rejuvenator, cordyceps is believed to be the best remedy for anaemia, body fluid loss, excessive fatigue, body aches and pains, moodiness and irritability. The herb is also believed to be excellent for strengthening the lung and aiding bone marrow development. Growing children and the elderly, in particular, will benefit from better overall health as its curative properties are so wide-ranging. It is prescribed for recovery from illnesses as it encourages appetite and builds up resistance against chills and colds. Widely used in stews and soups, cordyceps do not require any preparation before cooking.

   The Mandarin name of cordyceps literally translates into "worm in winter, grass in summer". Cordyceps is a species of fungi. In mid-autumn, the matured spores of this fungus are dispersed into the soil. The spores then penetrate the bodies of any bat moth larvae they encounter and the larvae bore into the soil for winter hibernation. Meanwhile, the spores invade every part of each larva and form hyphae after germination to feed on the larva. Gradually, the larva is consumed and filled with fungal mycelium, with only the outer skin intact. By now, the fungal mycelium structure resembles the pupa of a moth, which shrivels up in summer to look like a dried up twig. The 'twigs' are harvested as cordyceps.

Cuttlefish

Cuttlefish is sold in supermakets and provision shops where they come in dried, whole pieces between 12 and 15 cm long. Cuttlefish is often used to flavour soups but it is also high in cholesterol content, so avoid using large amounts.

   To prepare, remove eyes and hard, central bone, cut tentacles into half lengthways (lengthwise) and the rest into four pieces. Soak in water for five minutes, drain and wash off grit before cooking.

Dates

Dates are said to be effective in countering fatigue, anaemia and low energy levels, strengthening the stomach and spleen and soothing the heart and lungs. Traditionally, Chinese women undergoing confinement used a lot of dried dates in their diets to build up their strength and blood. In some preparations, whole dried dates are simmered in hot water until a thick liquid is obtained. In others, they are added to other herbs in tonic dishes to give a pleasant aroma and naturally sweet taste.

Of the various types, red dates (*hong zao / hung cho*) and black dates (*hei zao / hak cho*) are the most commonly used. There are also sweet dates (*mi zao / mut cho*) and southern dates (*nan zao / nam cho*). Sweet dates are dried dates that have been coated with honey and are also good for strength and vitality. Southern dates are actually nearly black in color and longish in appearance. They are reputedly the best and more costly.

To remove stones, use a sharp knife to slice the dates open. Alternatively, smash dates with the flat side of a cleaver, then remove exposed stones. Wash dates in some water and cook as required.

Donkey's glue (*e jiao / ah kau*)

Donkey's glue is a substance made from donkey skin. In the shops, donkey's glue comes in the form of brownish to black rectangular blocks. The blocks melt easily into a smooth and odourless liquid that is used to relieve stomach irritation, abdominal pains, chronic fatigue and moodiness. It is sometimes prescribed to counter malnutrition and the effects of tuberculosis.

Donkey's glue can also restore blood and check bleeding. Its gelatinous nature is believed to increase blood viscosity, which aids blood clotting in the event of gashes or other such wounds. Donkey's glue, however, has been established to contain much calcium, which is vital to the process of blood clotting.

Due to its wide-ranging medical benefits, donkey's glue is popularly brewed with herbs that nourish the nerves, restore energy and relieve such ailments as chronic fatigue, insomnia and anaemia.

Dried scallop (*gan bei / kong yue chee*)

A pricey ingredient, dried scallops are generally used as seasoning to impart a delicate flavour to dishes. Traditionally, they were available only from herbalists and sold by weight. Today, dried scallops are sold prepacked in some supermarkets.

There are a few ways of preparing dried scallops for use: first, soak scallops in a little cold water overnight before breaking them up; second, boil scallops or steam them in a little water until they break up; third, if you like the scallops on the crunchy side, soak in a little cold water for five minutes before use. In all three instances, save the liquid for cooking.

Eggs (chicken)

A very popular and basic ingredient in cooking, eggs are also a healthy food. They provide proteins, vitamins, minerals, and also some fat. The issue of cholesterol that builds up in our bodies from eating eggs and how that cholesterol contributes to heart disease is controversial. Here, as is the case with most other foods, moderation is key and overindulgence ill-advised.

In cooking, only the freshest of eggs should be used. To test for freshness, place the egg in a bowl of water. If it is fresh, it will lay horizontally on its side. If not, it will rest tilted at a semi-vertical position. If it is bad, it will pop into a completely vertical position.

Garlic

One of the most common kitchen herbs, garlic has many beneficial properties. It can tone up poor digestion by stimulating the digestive system with its antiseptic properties, regulate liver and gall bladder functions, lower blood pressure, counter arteriosclerosis and clear bronchitis.

Garlic has a pungent smell and flavour and too much of it can be overpowering and unbearable which is why some people have an aversion to it. Its concentrated flavour, and for which there is no substitute, however, does improve the taste of many dishes. Garlic should not be eaten excessively as it can become slightly toxic to the body. Overindulgence in garlic can lead to damage of the eyes, lungs and spleen.

Ginger

Ginger contains protein, vitamins A, B complex and C, calcium, phosphorus, iron, sodium, potassium and magnesium. It is also a heating and stimulating food that combats ailments relating to internal and external coldness. Ginger is popularly used to relieve colds, flatulence and colic. It helps to cleanse the system by inducing perspiration and in cases of food poisoning resulting from bad meats, promotes the expulsion of toxins from the body. Ginger improves appetite and digestion by stimulating the flow of saliva, helps to prevent vomiting and eases painful or problematic menstruation because of its *yang* properties.

Traditionally, Chinese mothers in confinement consumed a lot of ginger. Here, old ginger is used more often than young ginger because it is more heating. Malay mothers in confinement also put generous amounts of ginger in their food because they believe that ginger helps the uterus to contract.

In general, Asians use a lot of ginger in their cooking. The Indians drink ginger water boiled with rock sugar to cure coughs and colds, while the Chinese use it mainly to relieve themselves of wind, bloating and flatulence, and to induce warmth. It is common practice, for example, to add a few slices of young ginger to soups, stews and other dishes to remove any *yin* elements or elements of coldness they may contain.

Gingko nut (*bai guo* / *bak gor*)

Yellow nuts inside hard, beige shells, gingko nuts are usually used in sweet brews. Reputedly good for bladder ailments and urinary problems, it is also believed to relieve coughs and chest conditions. The nuts can be bought shelled or unshelled. The former, however, does not keep well.

Ginseng

For centuries, the Chinese have held ginseng in the highest esteem. The root is highly prized as a rejuvenator and for some, a panacea. In recent years, research has shown that the constituents in ginseng are exceedingly complex, consisting of saccharides, volatile oils, fatty oils, sterols, amino acids, alkaloids, saponins, cellulose and vitamins. The saponins (a mixture of 13 simpler ones), in particular, have special therapeutic effects on the human physiology.

Ginseng is known to reinforce vigour, help blood circulation, strengthen the heart and stabilise the nerves. It also cures ailments such as neurasthenia, debility, anaemia and limb fatigue. Frequent intake of ginseng is said to increase metabolism, refresh the mind, strengthen the physique and promote longevity. As a rejuvenator, ginseng encourages salivation and appetite, as well as tops up the body's energy level (due to its mildly stimulating effect on the central nervous system and other parts of the body). Some have gone as far as to treat it as an aphrodisiac. Ginseng, then, is excellent in aiding the physical and mental faculties of the elderly, frail children or those who suffer from general weakness. Due to its potency, however, only very little should be taken by this group of people and even then, mixed with gruel or honey.

Ginseng is divided into two main types — wild and cultivated, with wild ginseng always more valuable and valued. The wild ginseng of Kirin, China is considered among the best and is exorbitant in price but still much sought after. This is because it is supposed to be very old, probably over a century. The older the ginseng, the more effective it is believed to be and hence the more expensive. Into the twenty-first century, wild ginseng, while extremely expensive, is also quite rare and using cultivated ginseng is more or less the norm. Due to the success of past cultivation efforts, the growth period of ginseng has since been drastically shortened. In Kirin, it can take as few as six years from sowing to harvesting.

The more common categories of ginseng are Chinese (*ren shen* / *yan sum*), American (*yang shen* / *yong sum*) and Korean (*gao li shen* / *go lai sum*). Their names, however, are not indicative of where they have been cultivated, but their species. China, for example, is the world's largest producer of American ginseng. Within each species of ginseng are different grades, which determine the price you pay.

American ginseng is usually sold in three parts — the top 1 to 2 cm of the root, also known as the "head"; the bulk of the root, which can be bought whole or ready sliced; and the threadlike shreds that extend from the root, known collectively as the "beard". The shreds are not usually used for tonics or brews because they are the least effective of the ginseng grades. Instead, the shreds are used only for making mild teas (see *Aids for Common Ills*).

Korean ginseng, too, comes ready sliced or whole and tends to be used for simmering with meats and other ingredients. When buying whole, get the herbalist to cut it into thin slices for you.

Pau shen or *pau sum* is an expensive and sometimes controversial category of ginseng without an English equivalent in name. Some sources define *pau shen* as the best Chinese ginseng, while others define it in no uncertain terms as American ginseng. Still others say that *pau shen* refers not to the species of ginseng but to a particular, superior grade within each type of ginseng. *Pau shen* is rarely cooked in stews or tonic brews and is paired only with a select few ingredients such as bird's nest and hasima. It is more commonly brewed as a tea and appreciatively drunk on its own. It is only recommended to older children and adults.

Hasima (*xue ge* / *shuet kup*)

Glands of the northern Chinese snow frog, hasima cleanses and balances the system. It is also reputed to contribute to smooth skin. For the uninitiated, the taste of these little cotton ball-like clumps can be difficult to stomach. It has crunch, however, and when properly cooked, can be delicious. It is best to keep the quantity to a minimum as they swell considerably after cooking. To use, first remove veins, then soak in water for an hour or so.

Lily bulb petal (*bai he* / *bak hup*)

Herbalists sell dried lily bulb petals and recommend that they are added in small quantities to sweet brews. The petals are believed to relieve coughs and colds, as well as restore the body's internal balance.

Longan

Herbal shops mostly sell dried longan flesh, which is dark brown in colour. Some herbalists also sell dried whole longans, with shells and stones intact. These require considerable preparation before use.

Dried longan flesh is usually used in brews and teas for its warming and heat-inducing properties. It is especially indispensable in the diet of a new mother undergoing confinement.

Lotus root (*lian ou* / *leen ngau*)

The root of the lotus flower has a crunchy texture and is often used in soups. Lotus roots are cooling and are readily available in wet markets and supermarkets. To use, scrap off the outer layer, then slice into rings.

Lotus seed (*lian zi / leen chi*)

Seeds of the lotus flower are hard in texture and have a delicate flavour. Lotus seeds are cooling and often used in sweet and herbal brews. Lotus seeds can be bought dried or precooked. To prepare dried lotus seeds, soak in water for 5 to 10 minutes, drain, then boil in sufficient water for a few minutes. Remove skins and bitter cores if still intact. Precooked lotus seeds do not need preparation.

Marrow (*lao huang gua / lo wong kwa*)

The skin of this marrow, known to the Cantonese as "old cucumber", is coarse and brown. The vegetable has a good reputation for its cleansing and purifying properties. Marrow soups are excellent for neutralising toxic elements in the body arising from exposure to dust, dirt, grime, fumes and chalk particles. Many people in jobs subjected to these elements, eg quarry workers, office cleaners, factory workers, teachers and lorry drivers, consume this soup to counter the negative effects of those pollutants. Marrow is also an antidote for food poisoning resulting from eating fish or other seafood.

Mint

Mint leaves are used in a wide variety of ways — whether fresh, dried, crushed or ground and added to food, teas, soups, sauces or sweets. The versatile herb cools and soothes the body and is effective in easing flatulence, heartburn, cramps, abdominal pains and poor digestion, as well as activating perspiration. Headaches, migraines and vomiting due to nervousness also can be treated with mint, as can internal fevers, swellings and suppressed or painful urination.

Onion

Rich in vitamin C and an excellent diuretic, the onion stimulates the kidneys and promotes the flow of urine. Raw cut onions are effective in relieving pains from excess gas and heartburn but should only be consumed in moderate amounts. Onion soup, however, is recommended for a variety of ills. It relieves flatulence and common colds, whets the appetite, improves blood circulation and induces sleep.

Palm sugar (*gula melaka*)

This rich brown sugar comes in a round, compressed block and wrapped in leaves. To make palm sugar, sap from the flower-bearing shoots of the coconut palm is boiled, sieved and then left to stand until it crystallises.

For use in cooking, first unwrap the whole piece and wash to remove external grit, then portion the quantity required. As an added precaution, some people boil *gula melaka* in a little water before sieving the melted sugar. This is to remove any grit or other impurities that may have been trapped inside the solidified sugar block.

Peanut (groundnuts)

Peanuts impart a lot of goodness when boiled or steamed. They lubricate the lungs and stimulate the spleen. They also regulate the blood, act as a diuretic and improve the appetite. Try not to fry or roast peanuts or they become too heating.

Dishes cooked with peanuts or peanut roots are supposed to give strength and energy to growing bodies and children are often given peanut soups cooked in a variety of ways to encourage their growth. Some mothers do so specifically in the hope of making their children, especially the boys, grow taller.

To roast peanuts, put peanuts in a dry wok over very low heat. Stir continuously until peanuts are cooked through. Transfer to a flat, tray-like container and rotate while blowing gently at the peanuts to remove broken skin. Alternatively, transfer roasted peanuts to a cloth and rub together to remove skins.

Peppercorn

Pepper is as basic and commonly used as salt and there are many varieties to choose from, each one varying in aroma and pungency. White and black peppercorns are derived from the same plant — a vine of dark green leaves from which strings of berries hang. To produce black peppercorns, the berries are picked green and dried in the sun until they turn black. For white peppercorns, the berries are allowed to ripen before their orange-red skins and fleshy parts are removed to reveal the corns that are then dried.

Pigeon

Regarded as a heating food, pigeon is eaten to counteract and remove humidity from the body. As it is an excellent tonic for the blood, a person with a weak constitution or who suffers from impotence is often recommended a diet of pigeon. Pigeon is also believed to provide relief for irregular periods, skin sores and itchiness.

Potato

Potatoes are packed with carbohydrates and are a good source of starch and dextrin. Whenever possible, cook with the skin on since a good deal of nutrition is found near the skin. Potatoes that have been peeled but are not about to be cooked soon should be soaked in cold water to prevent darkening. Potatoes that have sprouted or are bearing greenish hues are toxic, so avoid using them.

Salt

This is one of the minerals essential to life. There is much value in salt. It brings out the flavour and taste of foods and soups and is a powerful preservative. Salt alleviates sore throats and reduces body heat. Those suffering from kidney diseases, oedema, hypertension, insomnia and asthma, however, should avoid taking salt.

Screwpine (*pandan*) leaves

Long and dark green in colour, screwpine leaves are usually added to sweets and desserts and impart a distinct and inimitable fragrance and flavour. To use, wash leaves well and use whole. Alternatively, tear each leaf into two lengthways (lengthwise), then tie each pair into a knot and add to dish. To extract juice, pound the leaves and squeeze for juice with a piece of muslin.

Sea cucumber (*hai shen* / *hoi sum*)

Also known as sea slugs or *beche-de-mer*, sea cucumbers are sold dried in herbal shops. Black in colour, each piece is shaped like a banana about 10 to 15 cm long. Considered a delicacy, they can be bought in their cleaned or uncleaned form and are said to be high in cholesterol so do not overindulge.

Sesame seed oil

Sesame seed oil is unsaturated and is an indispensable item when it comes to preparing food for mothers in confinement. It works to strengthen all organs in the body, especially the heart muscles, and nerves, as well as supply the body with oxygen. The oil imparts a strong, nutty fragrance and should be used sparingly.

Solomon's seal (*yu zhu* / *yok chok*)

Yellowish in colour, this herb is sold in thin, curly slices and is believed to be excellent for alleviating a host of ills, including throat and lung ailments. Do not wash before use.

Soy beans

The soy bean has hardly any carbohydrates or fat but is high in protein and fibre and contains potassium, phosphorous, calcium, iron, and vitamins A and B complex. No wonder, then, that this bean has been used in so many different ways and in so many different forms. The bean is used fresh, fermented or dried, or ground into a flour, and soy milk is a wonderful substitute for cow's milk. Below are some commonly used soybean-derived ingredients.

❖ Soybean paste (*dou jiang* / *dau cheong*) is made from preserved soybeans. To use, put the required amount into a small bowl and mash with a spoon until smooth. Salty in taste, the brown paste is usually sold in jars and imparts a strong, distinctive flavour to food.

❖ Bean curd (*dou fu* / *dau fu*) is a versatile ingredient and can be steamed, boiled, simmered, deep-fried or eaten fresh. Bean curd makes up for its blandness in taste by being a great flavour absorber. It is also easily digestible. There are two main types of bean curd — soft and hard — and both types are sold in squares. To prepare, wash in clean water, drain and cut into halves or quarters.

❖ Dried bean curd sticks (*fu zhu* / *fu chok*) are pale yellow in colour and have a crinkled appearance. Before cooking, they have to be broken into short lengths and soaked in water. They are ideal in both sweet and savoury soups.

❋ Red fermented bean curd (*nan ru / nam yue*) refers to reconstituted cubes of mashed fermented beans soaked in brine, wine, spices and chillies. They are sold in jars and used as a seasoning or condiment.

❋ Soy sauce, a popular seasoning in Chinese cooking, is made from fermented soy beans. This sauce comes in two main types: light and dark. Although it is rich in vitamins and minerals, it nevertheless contains about 18 per cent salt and so should be used sparingly.

Water chestnut

Water chestnuts are edible tubers which are used widely in oriental cooking. They are roundish, with a brown-blackish skin and firm, white flesh. A cooling food, they are popular also because they have a delicate nutty flavour and add crunch to a dish. They are available fresh from groceries or wet markets. To prepare for use, first soak water chestnuts in water, then scrub to remove grit and mud before peeling.

Watercress (*si yang cai / sai yong choy*)

A cooling vegetable, watercress can alleviate dry coughs, sore throats and irritability. Rich in iron, iodine, potassium and other minerals, watercress is also known to treat anaemia and stimulate glandular activity. Watercress is generally highly regarded for the prevention of illness and the restoration of health after an illness.

To avoid kidney problems, refrain from excessive or prolonged intake. Those with stomach upsets like diarrhoea should avoid it as well because it is cooling and can aggravate the condition. The juice of the vegetable should not be taken undiluted as it can lead to inflammation in the throat and stomach.

White fungus (*bai mu er / shuet yi*)

Also known as silver fungus (*yin er / ngan yi*), white fungus is clear as crystal and very attractive before it is picked. In the shops, white fungus is dried, hard and brownish-yellow in colour. When immersed in water, however, the dried pieces will swell up and regain their original colour. The fungus is elastic and tough in texture and retains its shape even after being stewed for hours.

White fungus is prescribed for a variety of ills. It can check irregular menstruation, enhance the body's gonadal functions, improve skin complexion, relieve ulcers and constipation and bring down fever.

White fungus can be prepared with different meats in dishes or soups. To use, soak in hot water for half an hour, then remove dirt and grit. As it is able to expand up to 12 times its original size, very little needs to be used in any dish.

Chinese ginseng

Korean ginseng

American ginseng

Bird's nest

Hasima

Cordyceps

Gecko

Codonopsis root

Astragalus root

Chinese angelica

Cnidium root

Chinese yam

Solomon's seal

Donkey's glue

Boxthorn fruit

White fungus

Dried lily bulb petals

Gingko nuts

Dried longan flesh

Red dates

Black dates

Sweet dates

Lotus seeds

Sugared winter melon strips

Buddha's fruit

Chrysanthemum

Cogongrass root

BABIES AND TODDLERS

NEW MOTHERS often face the problem of preparing nutritionally sound food that is also acceptable to their babies' taste. Babies can be both fussy and faddy in their choice of food. Although milk forms the main part of a baby's diet for the first year, solid foods will have to be introduced from about four months, when a baby's nutrient needs is no longer adequately met by milk alone. At this stage, other foods have to be included to ensure that the baby gets all the essential nutrients such as proteins, iron, vitamins and minerals to ensure healthy growth.

Most babies can be fed a spoonful or two of puréed vegetables, fruit, meat, and cereal from about four months. It is not until they are six to eight months old, however, that a wider variety of tastes and textures will begin to appeal to them. A broader range of vegetables (cabbage, cauliflower, celery, spinach, tomatoes, beans) and more solid foods, including potatoes, eggs, fish, meats, offal and soups, can be used in their meals when they grow more teeth and start to chew.

While the Western mother concocts mostly puddings, casseroles, purées, stews, loaves, creamed soups and baked and scrambled dishes, the traditional Asian mother usually falls back on a good number of broths, porridges and rice vermicelli dishes for their babies. In fact, broths are considered a staple in ensuring fit, healthy and bouncy babies.

Although meats, fish, chicken, eggs and vegetables are usually used to prepare baby fare, anchovies, dried scallops and dried oysters are favourite ingredients of indulgent mothers, grandmothers and baby minders when cooking for their charges. Animal fat, salt and sugar are food items that should be avoided in food for babies. When using meat, select the leanest possible cuts because fat is difficult for babies to digest. Salt can strain a baby's kidneys, and sugar can lead to tooth decay, cavities and other dental problems.

The recipe ideas that follow are both nourishing and palatable. In fact, their delicate and delicious flavours will go down well with older children and convalescents as well (who could resist a well-prepared, lip-smacking broth once in a while?). Conversely, older babies also can share some dishes at family meals. This introduces them to a wider and more interesting range of tastes, as well as a more balanced diet. A few spoonfuls of herbal soup or any restorative concoction cooked for the family can be served to a baby by itself or added to baby's porridge or rice. This is one way of putting junior on the right path to heavier brews and a healthier lifestyle in later life.

The quantities indicated are only guidelines. It is difficult to gauge how much food any one baby needs. Like adults, they have their hungry and not-so-hungry periods. Start with a spoonful or two to gauge the baby's likes and dislikes and do not force when refused. Generally, most babies will eat the amount they need. Tread carefully when introducing new foods. It is best to do so one at a time. This will make it easier to detect food allergies which can occur in babies under 12 months old. Steer clear of unsuitable foods that do not agree with the constitution of young babies. These include spicy dishes such as curries and acidic fruits such as green mangoes, pineapple and grapefruit.

Considering that babies have a lower germ resistance than adults, all equipment relating to preparing, cooking and serving food for babies should be thoroughly cleaned.

Foods to be cooked should also be at their freshest and cleanest. The nutritional needs of a baby do not decrease with entry into the toddler years. Research has indicated that, in fact, years one to three are important, formative ones and a balanced diet with high nutrient density is vital for a toddler's development during this active growth period. Hence, a toddler's diet should include meats, vegetables and fruit to provide proteins, carbohydrates, fats, minerals and vitamins.

Recipes

Stocks:
1. Stock for soups and other dishes p.50
2. Chicken stock p.50
3. Anchovy stock p.50

Main meals

Porridges and broths:
1. Mixed vegetable broth p.51
2. Liver porridge p.51
3. Fish porridge p.52
4. Dried oyster and fish porridge p.52
5. Dried scallop and anchovy porridge p.54
6. Sweet potato porridge p.54
7. Kidney bean and rice porridge (version 1) p.56
8. Kidney bean and rice porridge (version 2) p.56
9. Chicken congee p.58
10. Vegetable and chicken porridge p.58

Soups:
1. Fine rice vermicelli soup p.59
2. Egg drop soup p.60
3. Amaranth and egg soup p.60

Dishes:
1. Steamed omelette p.62
2. Eggah p.63
3. Steamed egg with bean curd p.63
4. Double-boiled eggs with minced pork p.64
5. Steamed minced pork with salted fish p.64

Sweets and Tonic Brews
1. Rice and milk pudding p.66
2. Steamed egg with milk p.66
3. Korean ginseng in rice water p.66

Stock for soups and other dishes

Serves 1–2

Soup stocks add more flavour and delicacy to baby foods. Since ordinary stock and stock cubes are too highly seasoned and salty for babies, it is best to prepare your own. Mutton bones can also be added.

Ham or beef bones	500 g
Pork spare ribs	500 g, excess fat trimmed
Dried oysters	6–8, soaked and grit removed
Dried scallops	4–6, soaked
Salt	$1/2$ tsp or more to taste
Water	2 l (8 bowls)

- ✧ Break bones and spare ribs.
- ✧ Combine all ingredients in a large, heavy-based saucepan. Add sufficient water to cover bones. Cover and bring to the boil. Simmer for 1–2 hours.
- ✧ Skim off oily scum from surface. Strain stock and leave to cool. Skim off fatty layer from surface of cooled stock.
- ✧ Use this stock as the base for soups and dishes. Refrigerate, use as required.

Chicken stock

Serves 1–2

Meaty chicken carcasses	2
Salt	$1/2$ tsp or more to taste
Water	2 l (8 bowls)

- ✧ Combine all ingredients in a large saucepan. Bring to the boil.
- ✧ Cover and simmer gently for $1^{1}/_{2}$–2 hours. Frequently skim off fat from surface.
- ✧ Remove from heat. Leave to cool. Refrigerate, use as required.

Anchovy stock

Serves 1–2

Anchovies	80 g, cleaned, soaked and drained
Water	2 l (8 bowls)

- ✧ Combine all ingredients in a large saucepan. Bring to the boil. Cover and simmer gently for $1^{1}/_{2}$–2 hours.
- ✧ Remove from heat. Discard anchovies and leave stock to cool. Refrigerate, use as required.

Porridges and broths

Mixed vegetable broth
Serves 1–2

Stock	1 l (4 bowls)	
Carrots	50 g, cleaned and diced	
Turnip	30 g, cleaned and diced	
Dried scallops	2, soaked to soften	
Dried oysters	4, soaked and grit removed	
Marrow (*lao huang kua* / *lo wong kwa*)	50 g, peeled, seeded and diced	
Watercress (*si yang cai* / *sai yong choy*)	50 g, washed and finely chopped	
Amaranth (*xian cai* / *yeen choy*)	50 g, washed and finely chopped	
Cucumber	50 g, thinly sliced	
Salt	1/2 tsp	
Crisp-fried shallots	for garnishing	
Sesame seed oil	for garnishing	

◈ Bring stock to the boil in a saucepan. Add carrots, turnip, scallops and oysters. Simmer over low heat for 20 minutes.

◈ Add marrow and watercress. Simmer for 10 minutes. Add amaranth and cucumber, then salt. Simmer for 5 minutes more. Remove from heat.

◈ Serve warm. Garnish with shallots and/or a few drops of sesame seed oil if preferred.

Liver Porridge
Serves 1–2

Sesame seed oil	1/2 tsp or more to taste
Shallots	2, chopped
Rice	120 g, washed and drained
Water or stock	1 l (4 bowls)
Lean pork	50 g, finely minced
Pig's liver	100 g, finely minced
Egg white	1, lightly beaten
Light soy sauce	1 tsp; replaceable with 1/4 tsp salt

◈ Heat sesame seed oil in a wok. Brown shallots. Remove from wok and set aside.

◈ Combine rice and water or stock in a pot. Boil for 20 minutes or until grains break. Reduce heat and simmer. Add sufficient water to achieve desired consistency.

◈ Add minced pork. Simmer for 3 minutes. Add liver, then egg white. Season with soy sauce or salt. Remove from heat.

◈ Serve with fried shallots or if you prefer, add 1 tsp sesame seed oil to porridge before removing from heat.

Tip

❖ Add pepper to taste and garnish with chopped spring onions (scallions) or coriander (cilantro) leaves if serving to older children or adults.

Fish porridge
Serves 1–2

Fish is a versatile food, rich in calcium and a good source of protein. Freshness is an important factor in the selection of fish whether cooking for babies or adults. After washing fish, clean hands with lime or tamarind juice to get rid of the smell. If threadfin is unavailable, replace with white pomfret meat. Although both types of fish are on the expensive side, they have smooth flesh and are tasty. They are best eaten steamed or cooked in porridges for babies.

Sesame seed oil	½ tsp or more to taste
Shallots	2, sliced
Rice	120 g, washed and drained
Water or stock	750 ml (3 bowls)
Threadfin	75 g, skinned and diced
Tomato	1, small; peeled, seeded and sliced
Ginger	1-cm knob, shredded
Light soy sauce	1 tsp; replaceable with ¼ tsp salt

- ✧ Heat sesame seed oil in a wok. Brown shallots. Remove from wok and set aside.
- ✧ In a pot, boil rice in water or stock for 20 minutes or until grains break. Adjust liquid amount to achieve desired consistency.
- ✧ In a bowl, mix fish, tomato, ginger, soy sauce and salt. Add mixed ingredients to pot. Stir well for 3 minutes. Add a few drops of sesame seed oil. Remove from heat.
- ✧ Discard ginger, then garnish with fried shallots if serving to babies.
- ✧ Garnish with coriander (cilantro) leaves and sliced spring onions (scallions) if serving to older children or adults.

Tips
- ❖ It is better to remove tomato skin and seeds as babies find these hard to digest.
- ❖ If you want your porridge to be of a smoother and creamier texture, like that sold by restaurants or good porridge stalls, add 1 pinch salt and 1 tsp oil to the washed and drained rice and leave to marinate for 5 to 10 minutes before adding water to boil. The cooking time here will be shorter.

Dried oyster and fish porridge
Serves 1–2

Rice	120 g, washed and drained
Stock or water	750 ml (3 bowls)
Dried oysters	8–10, soaked and grit removed
Tomato	1, small; peeled, seeded and sliced
Light soy sauce	1 tsp; replaceable with 1 pinch salt
Threadfin or white pomfret	100 g, skinned and diced
Sesame seed oil	1 tsp
Crisp-fried shallots	1 tsp

- ✧ Combine rice and stock or water in a small clay pot. Add oysters, tomato, and soy sauce or salt. Simmer over very low heat for 30 minutes.
- ✧ Add fish and sesame seed oil to simmering porridge. Sprinkle shallots on top. Simmer over low heat for 30 minutes more. Serve.

Tips
- ❖ Do not feed oysters to baby.
- ❖ Do not stir porridge at any stage of cooking.

Dried scallop and anchovy porridge
Serves 1–2

If your baby is a fussy eater and favours only flavourful and aromatic food, cook his or her rice porridges in a small clay pot. Cook over very low heat to prevent burning and simmer for one hour or slightly more. The resulting rice porridge will be tastier and have a smoother consistency because all the flavours would have been amply sealed in.

Rice	120 g, washed and drained
Water or stock	750 ml (3 bowls)
Dried scallops	4–6, soaked
Anchovies	25 g, cleaned and washed
Tomato	1, small; peeled and cut into wedges
Light soy sauce	1 tsp; replaceable with 1 pinch salt
Sesame seed oil	1 tsp
Crisp-fried shallots	1 tsp

✧ In a small clay pot, combine rice and stock or water. Except sesame seed oil and shallots, add all other ingredients. Simmer over very low heat for 30 minutes.
✧ Add sesame seed oil to simmering porridge. Sprinkle fried shallots on top. Simmer for 30 minutes more. Serve.

Tips
❖ Babies find anchovies difficult to chew, so unless one cares to pound them into a more digestible state, refrain from giving to children younger than 2$\frac{1}{2}$ or 3 years old. Scallops, on the other hand, break into small pieces after prolonged cooking. A baby of 15 months can safely chew and swallow very small pieces of scallops.
❖ Do not stir the porridge at any stage of the cooking process or the porridge texture will not be smooth.

Sweet potato porridge
Serves 1–2

Sweet potatoes have different coloured skins, from white to magenta to purple. Most of them are true to their name and taste sweet. They are excellent sources of vitamins A and C. In days past, sweet potato porridge was synonymous with poverty. As sweet potatoes were, and still are, cheaper than rice, chunks of the tuber were added to pots of thin rice porridge to inexpensively make a heartier meal for the family. Notwithstanding this tradition, many people find this combination interestingly different.

Sweet potato	1, average-size; peeled and cut into chunks
Rice	100 g, washed and drained
Stock or water	1 l (4 bowls)
Salt	$\frac{1}{2}$ tsp

✧ Combine all ingredients in a pot. Bring to the boil. Simmer for about 20 minutes or until grains break.
✧ Adjust liquid amount and simmer to achieve desired consistency. Eat with side dishes (see p.62–64).

Kidney bean and rice porridge (version 1)

Serves 1–2

This tasty and robust dish has not only a pretty colour, but also a high protein content.

Kidney beans	100 g, washed and drained
Stock	200 ml (³/₄ bowl)
Cooked rice	1 bowl
Tomatoes	3, small; peeled, seeded and sliced
Salt	¹/₄ tsp
Crisp-fried shallots	2 tsp

✧ Boil kidney beans in sufficient water until they soften and break. Adjust liquid amount to 250 ml (1 bowl) before adding stock, rice, tomatoes and salt. Bring to the boil. Simmer until well blended. Add shallots.

✧ Add pepper to taste if serving to adults.

Kidney bean and rice porridge (version 2)

Serves 1–2

Kidney beans	100 g, washed and drained
Salt	1 pinch
Rice	100 g, washed and drained
Water	1¹/₂ l (6 bowls)
Light soy sauce	1 tsp
Crisp-fried shallots	1 tsp

✧ Boil kidney beans in sufficient water for 5 minutes. Remove from heat. Let stand for 1 hour.

✧ Drain kidney beans. Add salt and sufficient fresh water. Bring to the boil. Simmer for 45–60 minutes or until soft. Drain and set aside.

✧ Combine rice and water in a pot. Cook over moderate heat for 30 minutes or until grains break. Add kidney beans. Mix well. Add soy sauce. Simmer over low heat for 10–15 minutes or until rice and beans are soft enough for baby.

✧ Garnish with shallots to serve. For adults, add pepper to taste.

Chicken congee

Serves 2

This dish should only be served to older toddlers.

Water	2 l (8 bowls)
Chicken	1, about $\frac{1}{2}$ kg; cleaned
Rice	200 g, washed and drained
Chicken stock cube (optional)	1, small
Salt	$\frac{1}{2}$ tsp
Light soy sauce	1 tsp
Sesame seed oil	1 tsp
Young ginger	4-cm knob, finely shredded
Spring onions (scallions)	3 stalks, finely chopped

- Bring water to the boil. Add chicken. Cover and cook for 15 minutes. When done, remove chicken and leave to cool. Reserve stock. Debone cooled chicken and save bones. Dice or shred chicken meat.
- In a large pot, combine $1\frac{1}{2}$ l (6 bowls) stock, chicken bones, rice and stock cube if used. Bring to the boil. Simmer over moderate heat for about 30 minutes or until grains are broken. Add more water to achieve desired consistency if necessary. Remove chicken bones. Add salt and soy sauce.
- To serve, garnish with shredded chicken meat and drizzle sesame seed oil on top.
- For adults, add ginger, spring onions and pepper to taste.

Vegetable and chicken porridge

Serves 1–2

Without the addition of chicken meat, this dish is suitable for vegetarians too.

Rice	120 g, washed and drained
Peanuts (groundnuts)	50 g, shelled
Water	1 l (4 bowls)
Soaked Chinese mushrooms	30 g, stems removed and finely shredded
Carrots	30 g, diced
Cabbage	30 g, finely shredded
Chicken meat	50 g, diced
Light soy sauce	1 tsp; replaceable with $\frac{1}{4}$ tsp salt or more to taste
Sesame seed oil	1 tsp

- Combine rice, peanuts and water in deep saucepan. Bring to the boil. Reduce heat and simmer for 30 minutes or until rice grains break.
- Add mushrooms and carrots. Simmer for 25 minutes. Add cabbage and chicken, then soy sauce. Simmer 5–10 minutes. Add water if porridge is dry.
- Serve with a few drops of sesame seed oil.
- Garnish with chopped spring onions (scallions) and pepper for older children and adults.

Soups

Fine rice vermicelli soup
Serves 2–3

Better known as *mee sua* in Hokkien or *meen seen* in Cantonese, these fine and fragile noodles are ideal for babies and people with digestive problems because of their soft texture after cooking. Preparing them takes dexterity, however, as one has to be very quick in scalding them, adding them to the prepared soup and then removing the lot one to two minutes later. Any longer and the noodles turn into unpalatable, starchy lumps.

Sesame seed oil	4 Tbsp
Shallots	4, sliced
Garlic	1 clove, chopped
Fresh prawns	6, diced
Stock or water	1¹/₂ l (6 bowls)
Fine rice vermicelli (*mian xian / meen seen*)	5 bundles
Diced threadfin	4 Tbsp
Egg white	1, well beaten
Spring onions (scallions)	2 stalks, chopped

◇ Heat 2 Tbsp sesame seed oil in a wok. Brown shallots. Remove from wok and set aside.
◇ Heat remaining oil. Add garlic and stir. When brown, add prawns. Add stock or water and simmer.
◇ Separately scald vermicelli in boiling water and drain. Add to wok together with fish. Stir in egg white and remove from heat immediately.
◇ To serve, garnish with spring onions. For adults, add pepper to taste.

Tips
❖ Fine rice vermicelli is usually on the salty side so add salt only after tasting.
❖ For variety, you can substitute prawn balls, fish balls and other vegetables for prawns and fish.

Egg drop soup

Serves 1–2

This recipe is possibly the simplest of soups. Also known as "egg flower soup" or "soup of the gods", this soup makes an excellent accompaniment to plain rice porridge or steamed rice, as well as fried rice.

Clear chicken stock	750 ml (1½ bowls)
Egg	1, well beaten
Spring onion (scallion)	1 stalk, finely chopped
Sesame seed oil	1 tsp
Salt to taste	

- Bring stock to the boil in a saucepan. Remove from heat.
- Drip beaten egg in a narrow stream along the prongs of a fork into the chicken stock, trailing it over the surface. Wait for 15 seconds for the egg to set before stirring. Add salt.
- Serve hot. Garnish with spring onion and drizzle sesame seed oil on top.

Amaranth and egg soup

Serves 1–2

The goodness of amaranth, or Chinese spinach, and egg soup is equalled only by its popularity.

Stock or water	1 l (4 bowls)
Minced chicken or pork	25 g
Amaranth (*xian cai / yeen choy*)	150 g, cleaned and hard stems removed
Egg	1, well beaten
Salt to taste	

- Pour stock or water into a saucepan. Stir in minced meat. Bring to the boil.
- Add amaranth. Pour egg in slow dribbles into centre of soup. Add salt to taste. Bring to the boil and sustain for 2 minutes. Serve hot.
- If serving to older children or adults, add pepper to taste.

Steamed omelette
Serves 2–3

Spring onion (scallion)	1 stalk, finely chopped
Minced lean pork or chicken (optional)	150 g
Light soy sauce	1 Tbsp
Eggs	4, well beaten
Water or chicken stock	250 ml (1 bowl)
Cooking oil for stir-frying	

✧ Heat a little oil in a wok. Stir-fry chopped spring onions for 30 seconds before adding meat. Fry for 5 minutes more. Add a little soy sauce. Transfer to a heatproof (flameproof) bowl.

✧ Separately combine remaining soy sauce, eggs and water or stock. Mix well. Pour egg mixture over fried meat. Steam for 15 minutes or until egg mixture is set.

Tips

❖ If not using meat, replace spring onion in recipe with 2 shallots, sliced. Fry shallots in 2 Tbsp oil until transparent. Add fried shallots to omelette before serving. If you prefer the omelette to be lighter, use 3 large eggs instead of 4.

❖ For adults, add 2 Tbsp sherry or other wine and/or a dash of sesame seed oil, as well as salt and pepper to taste to give the dish extra zest.

❖ In the past, when rice was cooked over a charcoal flame, the fuss-free way to prepare this dish involved placing the steaming bowl on top of the rice grains when they were about to cook. The heat from the steaming rice would sufficiently set the egg.

Eggah
Serves 1–2

Sesame seed oil	2 Tbsp
Shallot	1, finely chopped
Minced lean chicken, pork or beef	250 g
Salt	1 pinch
Eggs	3, well beaten
Potato	1, small; cooked and mashed
Stock or water	125 ml (1/2 bowl)

✧ Heat sesame seed oil in a wok. Stir-fry shallot. Add meat and fry until slightly brown. Remove from wok.

✧ Add remaining ingredients to fried meat. (Add pepper to taste as well if serving to adults.) Mix well. Pour mixture into a greased heatproof (flameproof) dish and cover.

✧ Lower heatproof dish into some boiling water in a pot. Double-boil for 30 minutes. When done, uncover and steam for a few minutes more or until egg is set. Serve hot.

Tip
❖ For eggah that is crispier or has a crustier top, grill the dish for a few minutes before serving.

Steamed egg with bean curd
Serves 1–2

Bean curd is inexpensive and nutritious. Because of its soft texture, babies and young children will find it easy to digest.

Soft bean curd	150 g, washed and cut into squares
Egg	1, beaten
Stock	125 ml (1/2 bowl)
Salt	1 pinch
Cooking oil	1/2 tsp
Minced meat or prawns (shrimps)	1 Tbsp
Sesame seed oil	1/2 tsp

✧ Put bean curd pieces into heatproof (flameproof) bowl. Set aside.

✧ Combine egg, stock and salt. Whisk well. Add oil. Pour mixture over bean curd. Add meat or prawns. Stir gently to mix well without breaking bean curd.

✧ Steam for 8–10 minutes. Drizzle sesame seed oil on top before serving.

Tip
❖ For adults, serve garnished with finely chopped spring onions and crisp-fried shallots. Add pepper to taste.

Double-boiled eggs with minced pork
Serves 1–2

Minced lean pork	250 g
Eggs (chicken)	2, well beaten
Salted (duck) egg	1, well beaten
Stock or water	125 ml (1/2 bowl)

Tip

❖ For variety, try adding some finely shredded young ginger and small pieces of salted fish on top of the dish when it is half cooked. Salted fish should be soaked and drained before frying in a little cooking oil until fragrant and crispy.

◇ In a bowl, combine minced meat and eggs. Mix well with stock or water. Add pepper to taste if serving to adults.

◇ Pour egg mixture into a heatproof (flameproof) bowl. Cover bowl and lower into some boiling water in a pot. Double-boil for 20 minutes or until egg mixture is set. Serve hot.

Steamed minced pork with salted fish
Serves 1–2

Although salted fish is not a commendable or nutritious food, when mixed with meat in small quantities, it adds that extra zest and pep that is likely to whip up the jaded appetite of a fussy eater. Knowledgeable mothers have been known to fry small pieces of salted fish until fragrant and crispy, and then pound them fine to sprinkle on top of porridges and soups for their children. Use only fleshy parts of salted fish and discard all bones. You can use either the Penang variety salted fish called *tahnau* or the Kuantan variety called *mui heong*.

Salted fish	60 g, cut into 4–5 pieces
Cooking oil	3 Tbsp
Minced lean pork	300 g
Water or stock	3 Tbsp
Pepper	1/2 tsp
Dark soy sauce	1 tsp
Light soy sauce	1 tsp
Young ginger	2-cm knob, cut into fine strips

◇ Soak salted fish in some water. Clean and drain well. Mince, then fry in a little oil until fragrant.

◇ Except ginger, combine all other ingredients in a heatproof (flameproof) bowl. Mix well until a smooth consistency is achieved. Sprinkle ginger strips on top. Steam for 20 minutes or until meat is done. Serve hot.

Tip

❖ Some people find that mixing salted fish with meat gives a fishy smell. They put the salted fish on top instead. For young children who cannot take ginger, remove the ginger strips before serving to them. The addition of pepper is said the give the dish a smoother consistency.

Rice and milk pudding
Serves 1–2

Pasteurised or UHT milk	125 ml (½ bowl)	✧ Add milk and salt to rice. Mix well. Set aside.
Salt	1 pinch	✧ Crack egg into a heatproof (flameproof) bowl. Add sugar.
Cooked rice	½ bowl	Beat well. Add milk mixture to beaten egg very slowly,
Egg	1	stirring continuously.
Sugar	1 tsp	✧ Put bowl into a saucepan of hot water over heat. Stir well
		until pudding thickens and is cooked. Serve warm.

Steamed egg with milk
Serves 1–2

Rock sugar	15 g, crushed	✧ Steam rock sugar until melted. Set aside.
Eggs	2, beaten	✧ Strain beaten egg into a mixing bowl to achieve a smoother
Milk	350–375 ml	consistency. Stir in milk. Add melted rock sugar. Mix well.
	(about 3	Pour into a heatproof (flameproof) bowl.
	bowls)	✧ Steam for 5–8 minutes. Remove from heat and serve.

Korean ginseng in rice water
Serves 1–2

Korean ginseng is generally acknowledged as a potent herb and very unsuitable for young members of the family. Some members of the older generations, however, advocate giving this potently stimulating brew to weak children between 10 months and four or five years of age, but in miniscule doses and only once in that age bracket, or at the most twice with a six-month gap. If yours are bouncing bundles of vitality, don't bother. If in doubt, don't even try. You can prepare this brew only when cooking rice, and the cooked rice will take on the fragrance of Korean ginseng.

Korean ginseng (*gao li shen* / *go lai sum*)	1–2 thin slivers	✧ Add an extra 50 ml (⅓ bowl) of water to the amount usually used to cook rice. When the water comes to a bubbly boil, transfer about 50 ml (⅓ bowl) of the water into a small, porcelain bowl.
Rice water	50 ml (⅓ bowl)	✧ Add ginseng slivers to bowl. Place bowl on top of rice grains. Replace rice cooker lid and do not remove until rice is cooked. When done, remove bowl of brew and leave to cool.
		✧ Feed 1–2 tsp to children, depending on age. The younger they are, the less they should imbibe.

THE GROWING YEARS
— Twelve Years and Under

PARENTS owe it to their children to supervise what they eat. This is especially important and critical during their growing years — a time when a lot of physical and mental energy is being used up at work (in school) and at play. As in the earlier stages of growth, what children eat today will determine their health in later years.

Surprisingly though, many parents pay greater attention to other aspects of their children's lives, eg academic pursuits and extracurricular activities, than to their diet. Children are so often fed fast food, instant noodles, hawker fare and canned food and parents do not realise that the wrong kinds of food served at daily meals can turn their children into nervous, anaemic or hyperactive bundles of unhappiness.

The syndrome of the hyperactive child, for example, is a common one. Such children are hot-tempered, tense, emotional, restless, on edge and cannot concentrate. They are easily excitable and irritable and are unable to maintain calm or composure when confronted with problems, let alone when faced with examinations. Hyperactivity has been medically acknowledged as a food illness. For some Chinese, this is thought to be due to overheating or overstimulation in the child's system through eating an excess of *yang* foods. Chocolate, coffee, fried potatoes (chips and crisps), deep roasted chicken, toasted and grilled foods, cocoa, and animal fat are stimulating foods. In the long run, these overload and create an imbalance in a young, growing body and cause the metabolic system to run faster than it should. An excess of such heating foods is also likely to lead to fevers, headaches, mouth ulcers, constipation and indigestion.

Balanced meals are important to growing children for healthy physical development and for recharging their batteries, maintaining reasonable reserves of energy to cope with the little ups and downs of growing up. Although all children are prone to bouts of coughs, colds, fever and chills, as well as fatigue, insomnia, irritability and aches, such ailments can be minimised if a balance of stimulating and calming foods are prescribed via herbal and tonic dishes. The restorative and preventive powers of these foods help children build up their organs and strengthen their nervous systems. Mothers who are firm believers of this school of thought are wont to carry on the tradition of their own mothers and grandmothers. To ensure the good health of their children, they prescribe with fervour a variety of nutritive, hearty soups and stews that have been enriched with a host of goodness-giving herbs. Time-tested favourites include boxthorn fruit (*gou qi zi / gei chi*) and carrot (for improving eyesight), onions (for relieving gas pains), watercress (for preventing illnesses), peanuts (for aiding growth), anchovies (high in protein) and soybean products. Since fluid is important to facilitating excrement and preventing dehydration, soybean milk, pearl barley water and chrysanthemum tea are commonly prescribed when hot weather prevails.

On no account, however, should growing children be dosed with potent herbs the likes of ginseng or Chinese angelica (*dang gui / dong kwai*). Such strong herbs may have adverse effects on their metabolism and upset their internal equilibrium. Stunted growth is commonly believed to result from this practice. It is even worse to give youngsters suffering coughs, colds, chills, ulcers and so on strong brews or heavy, heating soups involving double-boiled pigeons or meats. This, in fact, applies to both young and old. Most herbalists always dispense cautionary notes on this score but there are those who have been known to recommend ginseng for pregnant mothers or even toddlers.

If certain circumstances compel you to prescribe tonic nourishment, eg in the case of a child who has had a prolonged illness and is recovering, exercise much care and restraint in determining the dosage. Administering minimal doses of a double-boiled soup involving a sliver or two of ginseng and black chicken or bird's nest over a period of time, for example, will not cause undue harm. Otherwise, stick to safe and time-tested ingredients such as bird's nest, boxthorn fruit and the like.

You will notice that there are fewer recipes under *Dishes* here than in other sections. This is because children of this age generally can eat what is prepared for the rest of the family under the *Adolescence to Adulthood* section. Younger children who have not acquired a tasted for hot or spicy dishes can have ingredients like ginger, spring onions and peppers reduced or omitted.

Recipes

Main meals

Soups:
1. Clear chicken soup p.72
2. Onion, carrot and potato soup p.72
3. Watercress soup p.73
4. Winter melon soup p.73
5. Peanut and pork rib soup p.73
6. Bean curd and quail's egg soup p.74
7. Lotus root with dried cuttlefish soup p.74
8. Steamed chicken with mushroom soup p.76
9. Peanut root and pork rib soup p.76
10. Chicken, Chinese yam and boxthorn fruit soup p.76
11. Boxthorn leaves in soup p.78
12. Hasima and chicken soup p.78
13. Chicken, pickled radish and peanut soup p.78
14. Chicken, dried scallop and dried oyster soup p.80
15. Mushroom and quail's egg soup p.80

Dishes:
1. Bean curd and vegetable hotpot p.81
2. Stir-fried spinach p.82
3. Scallops and bean curd p.82

Sweets and Tonic Brews

Sweets:
1. Soybean and agar-agar jelly p.84
2. Pearl barley, lotus seeds, lily bulb petals, agar-agar p.84
3. Pearl barley, gingko nuts, lily bulb petals and lotus seeds p.85
4. Double-boiled egg custard p.85
5. Hasima with *pau sum* ginseng and red dates p.86
6. Black glutinous rice with coconut milk p.88
7. Sweet peanut porridge p.88

Tonic brews:
1. Double-boiled pig's brain with *keen fook san* p.90
2. Double-boiled chicken with codonopsis root p.90
3. Frog's legs and cordyceps soup p.91
4. Double-boiled bird's nest and *pau sum* ginseng p.91
5. Chicken with cordyceps p.91

Sweet brews:
1. Sugar cane and water chestnut tea p.92
3. Pearl barley water p.92
5. Lotus seeds, longan, Solomon's seal and barley p.92
2. Soybean milk p.94
4. Buddha's fruit with winter melon p.94
6. Double-boiled eggs with red dates p.95
7. Quail's eggs with red dates p.95
8. Five treasures brew p.95

Soups

Clear chicken soup
Serves 4–6

Free range chickens are said to be the best for this soup, which counters general debility caused by
common ills such as coughs and colds.

Soup:

Chicken	1, 1–1½ kg
Potatoes	200 g, peeled and quartered
Onion	1, large; peeled and halved
Peppercorns	½ tsp
Salt	1 tsp
Water	2 l (8 bowls)
Ginger	2-cm knob, thinly sliced
Pepper to taste	

Garnish:

Spring onions (scallions)	3 stalks, finely chopped
Crisp-fried shallots	2 Tbsp
Sesame seed oil	1 tsp

❖ Clean chicken. Discard head, neck and legs. Skin, then cut into large pieces.
❖ Except ground pepper, combine all other soup ingredients in a pot. Simmer for 1–1½ hours. Add pepper to taste. Serve hot.
❖ To serve, garnish with spring onions and shallot slices, then drizzle sesame seed oil on top.

Tip

❖ For bulk, you can add transparent vermicelli (*fen si / fun see*) to this dish. Soak in water and add to the soup 5 minutes before removing from heat.

Onion, carrot and potato soup
Serves 4–6

Many children have grown up with this nourishing soup. Onions contain a moderate amount of vitamin C and minerals, as well as help to improve appetite and blood circulation. Carrots are one of the richest sources of vitamin A, which is necessary for good eyesight and bone formation. They also contain some vitamin C and a good supply of minerals. Potatoes, lastly, are a good source of carbohydrates, starch and dextrin.

Chicken	1, about 1 kg
Chicken feet	4, talons cut off and scaly skins removed
Carrots	3, large; cut into chunks
Celery	2 sticks, diced
Potatoes	3, large; peeled and diced
Onions	2, large; peeled
Tomatoes	5–6, small and not too ripe; cut into wedges
Peppercorns	1 tsp, crushed
Salt	½ tsp or more to taste
Chicken stock	2 l (8 bowls)

❖ Clean chicken. Discard head, neck and legs. Skin if preferred. Cut into large pieces.
❖ Combine all ingredients in a big saucepan. Bring to the boil. Lower heat and simmer for 2–3 hours. Serve hot.

Watercress soup

Serves 4–6

Rich in vitamins A and C and various minerals, watercress contains the most iron after spinach (*bo cai /
bor choy*). An excellent brew for the liver and improved blood circulation, this soup helps to clear the
lungs and relieve congestion. Most Chinese mothers prescribe it warm at dinnertime.

Watercress (*si yang cai / sai yong choy*)	250 g
Water or stock	2 l (8 bowls)
Pork spare ribs or chicken	250 g, cut into desired serving-size pieces
Salt and pepper to taste	

✧ Discard roots and hard stems of watercress.
   Wash well and drain.
✧ Bring water or stock to the boil in a saucepan.
   Add spare ribs or chicken. Simmer for
   10 minutes.
✧ Add watercress. Simmer for 30–45 minutes.
   Add salt and pepper to taste. Serve hot.

Winter melon soup

Serves 4–6

Winter melon	1, medium-size; peeled, seeded and cut into rings
Pork ribs	350 g, cut into 3-cm pieces
Ginger	3-cm knob, sliced
Dried oysters	12, soaked and cleaned
Dried Chinese mushrooms	6, soaked, stems removed and finely sliced
Water or stock	2 l (8 bowls)
Salt and pepper to taste	

✧ Combine all ingredients in a pot.
   Simmer for 2–3 hours or until
   melon rings are soft. Add salt and
   pepper to taste. Serve hot.

Peanut root and pork rib soup

Serves 4–6

The roots of peanut plants are known to be very strengthening. Many mothers believe that regular
consumption of this soup will add inches to growing children and give them strong muscles.

Peanut (groundnut) roots	250 g
Pork ribs	250 g, cut into desired serving-size pieces
Water	2 l (8 bowls)
Light soy sauce	2 Tbsp
Salt	1/2 tsp or more to taste

✧ Peanut roots are difficult to clean thoroughly
   because soil clings to them. Soak and drain
   many times to remove all dirt and grit.
✧ Combine all ingredients in a pot. Simmer 2–3
   hours. Serve hot.

Tip
❖ If you prefer, chicken feet can be used instead of pork ribs.

Bean curd and quail's egg soup

Serves 4–6

This dish is high in protein and excellent for growing children. Both bean curd and quail's eggs are rich sources of protein.

Cooking oil	2 Tbsp
Shallots	2, large; sliced
Garlic	1 clove, crushed
Water or stock	1 l (4 bowls)
Salt	1/2 tsp
Dried Chinese mushrooms	6, soaked, stems removed and finely sliced
Fresh prawns (shrimps)	50 g, shelled and diced
Quail's eggs	20, hard-boiled and shelled
Soft bean curd	3 pieces, halved or quartered
Pepper to taste	
Spring onions (scallions)	2 stalks, finely chopped

- ◇ Heat 1 Tbsp oil in a wok. Fry half the shallots until crisp. Remove from wok and set aside.
- ◇ Add remaining oil to wok. Fry garlic until fragrant. Add remaining shallots. Fry for 1 minute. Transfer to a saucepan.
- ◇ Add water or stock and salt. Bring to the boil. Add mushrooms, prawns, quail's eggs and bean curd. Simmer for 4–5 minutes. Add pepper to taste.
- ◇ Serve hot. Garnish with spring onions and fried shallots.

Lotus root with dried cuttlefish soup

Serves 4–6

Dried cuttlefish	3 pieces
Fresh lotus roots	2, peeled and cut into 1/2-cm thick rings
Pork ribs	200 g
Dried oysters	6, soaked and cleaned
Dried scallops	3, soaked
Ginger	2-cm knob, crushed
Light soy sauce	1 tsp
Water	2 l (8 bowls)
Salt and pepper to taste	

- ◇ Wash cuttlefish. Discard eyes and hard, central bone of each piece. Cut each set of tentacles in half lengthways (lengthwise). Cut remaining parts into small pieces.
- ◇ Except salt and pepper, combine all ingredients in a pot. Cook over medium heat until lotus root changes colour and is slightly soft. Add salt and pepper to taste. Serve hot.

Tip

- ❖ Streaky pork can be used instead of pork ribs. When the soup is ready, remove pork, slice it and return to soup. Alternatively, serve separately with 1/2 tsp of light soy sauce drizzled over the top. If you find the boiled lotus root too bland, remove from soup, drain well and stir-fry for 2–3 minutes with 1–2 cloves of garlic and shallots for a crunchier texture. Serve with soup.

Steamed chicken with mushroom soup

Serves 4–6

Dried Chinese mushrooms combine well with meats and impart to the dish a distinctive aroma and flavour. Mushrooms are also a rich source of minerals.

Chicken	1, about 1 kg
Salt	1/2 tsp
Dried Chinese mushrooms	12–15, soaked and stems removed
Ginger	4-cm knob, shredded
Water	1 l (4 bowls)
Spring onions (scallions)	2 stalks, finely chopped

Tip
❖ If you prefer boiled soups, simmer for 2–3 hours instead.

❖ Clean chicken. Discard head, neck, legs and excess fat. Cut into large pieces. Rub all over with salt.
❖ Except spring onions, combine all other ingredients in a deep heatproof (flameproof) bowl. Steam over low heat for 45–60 minutes.
❖ Serve hot. Garnish with spring onions.

Peanut and pork rib soup

Serves 4–6

The goodness of peanuts can never be over extolled and it helps that young children generally enjoy eating softened peanuts. This soup is reputed to aid growth.

Raw shelled peanuts (groundnuts)	250 g
Pork ribs	200 g, cut into desired serving-size pieces
Dried oysters	6, cleaned and soaked
Light soy sauce	2 Tbsp
Salt	1/2 tsp or more to taste
Chicken stock or water	2 l (8 bowls)

❖ Combine all ingredients in a pot. Bring to the boil. Simmer for 2–3 hours. Serve hot.

Chicken, Chinese yam and boxthorn fruit soup

Serves 4–6

This delicious, aromatic soup is excellent for growing children. It replenishes their energy, improves their eyesight and aids their muscle and tissue growth. If you prefer, use two chicken carcasses instead of one whole chicken.

Chicken	1, about 1 kg
Dried scallops	6, soaked and drained
Chinese yam (*shan yao / wai san*)	30 g
Boxthorn fruit (*gou qi zi / gei chi*)	3 heaped Tbsp
Salt	1/2 tsp or more to taste
Water	2 l (8 bowls)

❖ Clean chicken. Discard head, neck and legs. Skin, then cut into large pieces.
❖ Combine all ingredients in a saucepan. Simmer for 3–4 hours. Serve hot.

Boxthorn leaves in soup

Serves 4–6

Young shoots and leaves from the boxthorn or Chinese wolfberry tree are often used as cooked greens
and are easily available in most Asian markets. The leaves help to combat eyestrain and contribute to
good vision. They are also said to be a tonic for the liver and kidneys.

Boxthorn leaves (*gou qi cai / gau gei choy*)	200 g
Stock (preferably anchovy)	1½ l (6 bowls)
Fish balls	12
Sesame seed oil	1 tsp
Crisp-fried shallots	2 Tbsp
Salt and pepper to taste	

❖ Discard stalks of boxthorn leaves. Cut leaves into smaller pieces. Wash well and drain.

❖ Bring stock to the boil in a saucepan. Add leaves and fish balls. Add salt and pepper to taste. Bring to another boil. Add sesame seed oil.

❖ Pour into serving bowls. To serve, sprinkle shallot slices on top.

Hasima and chicken soup

Serves 4–6

Hasima cleanses the body and balances the constitution. It is also reputed to contribute to smooth skin.
Keep the amount of hasima to a minimum so the resulting soup is clear and palatable, as well as
pleasing to the eye.

Hasima (*xue ge / shuet kup*)	50–60 g
Chicken thighs	2, skinned and excess fat removed
Salt	½ tsp or more to taste
Light soy sauce	1 tsp
Water	1½ l (6 bowls)
Pepper to taste	

❖ Remove veins on hasima. Soak in water for 1 hour. Drain well. Separate pieces so they do not clump together to become stodgy lumps when cooked.

❖ Except pepper, combine all other ingredients in a saucepan. Simmer over low heat for 2–3 hours. Add pepper to taste. Serve hot.

Chicken, pickled radish and peanut soup

This recipe makes an invigoratingly hearty and delicious soup for growing children.

Chicken fillet	250 g
Pickled radish (*da tou cai / dai tau choy*)	200 g, washed and sliced into 3-cm thick pieces
Shelled raw peanuts (groundnuts)	200 g
Salt	1 tsp
Water	2 l (8 bowls)

❖ Combine all ingredients in a large saucepan. Bring to the boil. Simmer for 2–3 hours. Serve hot.

Tip

❖ For variety, substitute chicken and pickled radish with 15–18 chicken feet. The combination of peanuts and chicken feet is said to strengthen weak legs and is also a health tonic for well being. To prepare chicken feet, remove scaly outer skins, cut off talons, wash a few times after rubbing with salt and drain. Some markets sell cleaned chicken feet.

Chicken, dried scallop and dried oyster soup

Serves 4–6

This recipe makes a clear and tasty soup that has traditionally delighted children. If you prefer, use three to four chicken breasts instead of one whole chicken.

Chicken	1, about 1½ kg
Dried scallops	12, soaked and drained
Dried oysters	20–25, cleaned, soaked and drained
Salt	½ tsp or more to taste
Peppercorns	1 tsp
Water	2 l (8 bowls)
Spring onions (scallions)	2 stalks, finely chopped

✧ Clean chicken. Discard head, neck and legs. Skin, then cut into large pieces.
✧ Except for spring onions, combine all other ingredients in a saucepan. Simmer for 3–4 hours.
✧ Serve hot. Garnish with spring onions.

Mushroom and quail's egg soup

Serves 4–6

Quail's eggs are rich in protein and, thus, good for growing children. Quail's eggs and mushrooms together make a tasty, flavourful dish. Dried Chinese mushrooms impart a strong flavour to the dish to which they have been added so use only the amount necessary when cooking soups or stews. If you prefer, Chinese flowering cabbage (*cai xin / choy sum*) can be used instead of amaranth.

Stock	750 ml (3 bowls)
Lean pork or beef	100 g, thinly sliced
Dried Chinese mushrooms	6, soaked, stems removed and thinly sliced
Canned button mushrooms	½ bowl
Carrot	1, cleaned and cut into small pieces
Amaranth (*xian cai / yeen choy*)	200 g, cut into 3-cm lengths
Quail's eggs	18, hard-boiled and shelled
Salt	½ tsp or more to taste
Pepper to taste	

✧ Bring stock to the boil in a saucepan. Add meat, mushrooms and carrot. Bring to another boil. Simmer for 10 minutes. Add amaranth, eggs, salt and pepper. Bring to the boil once more. Remove and serve.

Dishes

Bean curd and vegetable hotpot
Serves 4–6

Water or stock	1¹/₂ l (6 bowls)
Canned bamboo shoots	50 g, drained and thinly sliced
Dried Chinese mushrooms	15, soaked, stems removed and thinly sliced
Dried cloud ear fungus (*yun er / wun yi*)	50 g, soaked and cut into bite-size pieces
Carrots	2, small; thinly sliced
Cauliflower	75 g, cut into bite-size pieces
Soft bean curd	6 pieces, halved or quartered
Lean pork	150 g, thinly sliced
Dried lily buds (golden needles)	15 g, hard bits cut off, individually knotted, soaked and then queezed of excess water before use
Light soy sauce	1 Tbsp
Rice wine	2 Tbsp
Salt	¹/₂ tsp or more to taste
Pepper to taste	
Spring onions (scallions)	2 stalks, finely chopped

✧ Bring water or stock to the boil. Add bamboo shoots, mushrooms, fungus, carrots, cauliflower, bean curd and pork. Simmer for 15 minutes.

✧ Except for spring onions, add remaining ingredients. Simmer over very low heat for 10 minutes more.

✧ Serve hot. Garnish with spring onions.

Stir-fried spinach
Serves 4–6

Made famous by the cartoon character Popeye, this nutrient-rich vegetable is soft-textured and easily digested, especially for children who have an aversion to eating greens.

Cooking oil	3 Tbsp
Garlic	1/2 clove, crushed
Prawns (shrimps)	100 g, shelled
Spinach (*bo cai / bor choy*)	500 g, cleaned, old and withered parts removed and cut into 3-cm lengths
Light soy sauce	1 tsp
Salt to taste	
Cornflour (cornstarch)	1 tsp, mixed with 2 Tbsp water

✧ Heat oil in a wok. Add garlic. Stir-fry until fragrant. Add prawns, then spinach, soy sauce and salt. Stir well. Cover and simmer for 3 minutes.
✧ Add cornflour mixture to thicken. Stir for 1 minute more. Remove and serve.

Scallops and bean curd
Serves 4–6

Scallops impart a delightfully light and fresh flavour to an otherwise bland bean curd. This dish is delicious and healthy.

Dried scallops	8–10, soaked
Cooking oil	2 Tbsp
Shallots	2, finely sliced
Soft bean curd	4–5 pieces, quartered
Fresh young ginger	3–4 slices
Chinese cooking wine (*hua tiao / fa dew*)	1 Tbsp
Light soy sauce	1 tsp
Salt and pepper to taste	
Spring onion (scallion)	1 stalk, thinly sliced
Sesame seed oil	1/2 tsp

✧ Drain scallops and save liquid. Shred scallops and put into a heatproof (flameproof) dish. Add 250 ml (1 bowl) scallop liquid. Steam for 30 minutes. Drain scallops and save steamed liquid.
✧ Heat oil in a wok. Add shallots. Stir-fry until fragrant. Add bean curd, ginger and scallops. Add steamed scallop liquid and wine. Simmer for 5–8 minutes. Add soy sauce, salt and pepper to taste. Remove from heat.
✧ To serve, garnish with spring onion and sesame seed oil.

Sweets

Soybean and agar-agar jelly

This versatile combination of two nutritious foods makes for a delicious sweet, a nice change from the usual agar-agar with coconut milk jelly. Homemade soybean milk is always preferred, although readymade soybean milk can be substituted if in a hurry.

Agar-agar	25 g, soaked to soften
Soybean milk	1 ½ l (6 bowls)
Screwpine (*pandan*) leaves	4, each pair knotted together
Sugar	75 g
Vanilla essence (extract)	1 tsp

✧ Combine agar-agar, soybean milk and screwpine leaves in a saucepan. Cook over low heat. Stir until agar-agar dissolves.
✧ Add sugar and cook until completely dissolved. Add vanilla essence. Stir well. Remove from heat. Pour into jelly moulds. Refrigerate.

Pearl barley, lotus seeds, lily bulb petals and agar-agar

Pearl barley refers to barley kernels that have been hulled. Most provision shops and supermarkets sell pearl barley prepacked in cans or packets.

Pearl barley	50 g, washed
Precooked lotus seeds	50
Dried lily bulb petals (*bai he / bak hup*)	50 g
Agar-agar	25 g, soaked to soften
Water	2 l (8 bowls)
Rock sugar	150 g

✧ Except for rock sugar, combine all other ingredients in a big saucepan. Simmer over low heat for 45 minutes.
✧ Add rock sugar. Simmer 10 minutes more. Remove from heat and serve.

Pearl barley, gingko nuts, lily bulb petals and lotus seeds

Pearl barley	25 g
Gingko nuts (*bai guo / bak gor*)	40, shelled
Dried lily bulb petals (*bai he / bak hup*)	50 g
Precooked lotus seeds	50
Water	2–2$^1/_2$ l (8–10 bowls)
Rock sugar	150 g

❖ Except for rock sugar, combine all other ingredients in a saucepan. Simmer for 45 minutes. Add rock sugar. Simmer for 10 minutes more. Serve hot.

Double-boiled egg custard
Serves 4–6

Milk gives a delicious lip-smacking taste to this dish, which is known in Cantonese as *dun dan*. Water can be substituted for milk.

Rock sugar	150–200 g, steamed in 125 ml ($^1/_2$ bowl) water until melted
Eggs	6, large; well whisked
Fresh or evaporated milk	375 ml (1$^1/_2$ bowls)

❖ Pour cooled melted sugar into whisked eggs little by little, whisking continuously. Taste for desired sweetness.

❖ Slowly stir in milk. Stir only in one direction to achieve a smooth consistency. Make sure also that there are no air bubbles.

❖ Pour mixture into a double-boiler or deep heatproof (flameproof) bowl. If using the latter, double-boil in a wok or saucepan until custard sets. To test, insert a toothpick which should come out clean.

❖ To serve, scoop out onto serving dishes. It should have the consistency of soft bean curd.

Tips

❖ Alternatively, double-boil egg mixture in smaller heatproof (flameproof) serving bowls. This takes a shorter time, about 3–5 minutes. If preferred, add a few drops of screwpine (*pandan*) juice for added flavouring, as well as to mask the eggy smell. To obtain juice, wash 4 screwpine leaves, split each lengthways (lengthwise) and cut into 2-cm lengths. Then, pound leaves and squeeze with muslin cloth for about $^1/_2$ tsp juice.

❖ For a 'heatier' egg custard, omit the milk and add ginger juice. To obtain juice, pound 2 4-cm knobs of ginger to extract 2–3 tsp juice. Add to egg mixture, top up with 250 ml (1 bowl) water before double-boiling.

Hasima with pau sum ginseng and red dates

This is the sweeter, dessert version of cooking hasima. It is a tastier and lighter brew and can be served either hot or cold. Again, keep the quantity of hasima to a minimum. *Pau sum* ginseng can be omitted if you do not like the herby smell or taste, although it does add to the nutrition of the dish. The addition of screwpine leaves helps to mask the strong taste.

Hasima (*xue ge / shuet kup*)	50–60 g
Dried red dates (*hong zao / hung cho*)	20, stones removed
Gingko nuts (*bai guo / bak gor*)	30, shelled
Precooked lotus seeds	50
Pau sum ginseng	4–6 pieces
Rock sugar	100 g
Screwpine (*pandan*) leaves (optional)	2, knotted together
Water	2 l (8 bowls)

✧ Remove veins on soaked hasima. Soak for 1 hour more. Drain well before use.

✧ Combine all ingredients in a pot. Simmer for 3–4 hours. Serve hot or cold.

Black glutinous rice with coconut milk

Serves 4–6

Black glutinous rice is strongly believed to build up blood and strengthen the heart. This is a favourite dessert in Southeast Asia and is usually served with thick coconut milk, also known as coconut cream. Ensure that the black glutinous rice you use is of good quality as this makes a difference to the taste.

Black glutinous rice (*pulut hitam*)	250 g, washed, soaked in water overnight and drained
White glutinous rice	2–3 Tbsp, washed and drained
Water	2½ l (10 bowls)
Screwpine (*pandan*) leaves	4, knotted in pairs
Palm sugar (*gula melaka*)	2 whole pieces, soaked in a little boiled water and strained
Thick coconut milk	375 ml (1½ bowls), squeezed from 1 grated coconut and sufficient water
Salt	1 pinch

❖ Combine glutinous rices, water and screwpine leaves in a pot. Boil until rice is soft. Add sugar. Stir well for 2–3 minutes. Turn off heat.
❖ Separately bring coconut milk to the boil over low heat in a saucepan. Add salt. Remove from heat. Serve hot or cold.
❖ To serve, portion glutinous rice porridge into individual serving bowls. Top with 1–2 Tbsp coconut milk.

Tips
❖ If you are using a cooking method that incurs little to no evaporation, reduce liquid amount by 500 ml (2 bowls).
❖ Health conscious cooks can replace the freshly squeezed coconut milk used in this recipe with the prepacked, low-fat variety.

Sweet peanut porridge

Serves 4–6

Pound for pound, peanuts are more nutritious than meat or dairy products. This has proven to be a popular dessert.

Peanuts (groundnuts)	200 g, toasted in the oven or a dry pan until cooked through and skins removed
Sesame seeds	2½ Tbsp, toasted in a dry pan over low heat until golden brown
Water	2 l (8 bowls)
Sugar	125 g
Cornflour (cornstarch)	4 Tbsp
Evaporated milk or thick cream	250 ml (½ bowl)

❖ Combine peanuts, sesame seeds and 250 ml (1 bowl) water in a blender (processor) until smooth. Strain mixture to remove larger peanut bits.
❖ Bring sugar and remaining water to the boil. Add blended mixture. Stir well until smooth and creamy.
❖ Mix cornflour and evaporated milk or thick cream with 2 Tbsp water. Stir cornflour mixture into peanut porridge. Beat well until consistency thickens. Remove and serve.

Tips
❖ To remove skins of peanuts, gently blow at toasted peanuts to remove skins. If skins prove stubborn, transfer peanuts onto a clean cloth, rub them against each other through cloth, then blow at peanuts.
❖ Health conscious cooks could substitute the evaporated milk or thick cream for low-fat alternatives.

Double-boiled pig's brain with keen fook san
Serves 2–3

According to the theory of organotherapy, consuming pig's brain is good for stimulating one's grey matter and this preparation is said to help one's brain, especially a child's, to function at peak level. To prepare pig's brain, much care and patience is required. Extremely delicate and with a pudding-like texture, pig's brain will break into little pieces if one is not gentle in the cleaning process. First, soak in water for 30 minutes, then rinse many times. Remove veins if preferred; use a toothpick or cocktail stick to pick up one end of vein and roll up. When done, rinse until last change of water is clear. *Keen fook san* is a herb that helps to dispel the smell or taste of the brain that children may find hard to stomach. You should obtain *keen fook san* only from the herbalist, telling him or her that you require an amount enough for a dish serving two to three persons.

Pig's brain	1, thoroughly cleaned	✧ Combine all ingredients in a double-boiler or heatproof (flameproof) bowl. Double-boil over low heat for 4 hours.
Keen fook san	1 presciption	
Water	1 l (4 bowls)	
Shallots	3–4, peeled and left whole	
Salt	1/2 tsp	✧ At the end of cooking time, liquid amount should have reduced by at least 1/4 to leave about 750 ml (3 bowls) water; *keen fook san* absorbs water. Remove *keen fook san* before serving.
Peppercorns	1/2 tsp, crushed	

Double-boiled chicken with codonopsis root
Serves 4–6

Codonopsis root is popularly prescibed to children for improved blood circulation, as well as to counteract extreme mental and physical fatigue. If serving this soup to children, omit the Chinese cooking wine.

Chicken	1, about 1 kg	✧ Clean chicken. Discard head, neck and legs. Cut into large pieces.
Ginger juice	3 Tbsp	
Chinese cooking wine (*hua tiao / fa dew*)	2 Tbsp	✧ Season chicken with ginger juice and wine. Leave for 30 minutes.
Codonopsis root (*dang shen / dong sum*)	50 g	✧ Combine all ingredients in a double-boiler or heatproof (flameproof) bowl. Double-boil for 4 hours. Serve hot.
Chicken stock	1 1/2 l (6 bowls)	
Salt	1/2 tsp	

Frog's legs and cordyceps soup

Serves 4–6

This soup aids growth and good health by banishing appetite loss.

Fresh frog's legs	6–8, skinned	✧ Combine all ingredients in a saucepan. Simmer for 3 hours. Drink soup only.
Cordyceps *(dong chong xia cao / tung chung cho)*	30 g	
Ginger	2-cm knob, finely sliced	
Water	1¹/₂ l (6 bowls)	
Salt	¹/₂ tsp	
Pepper to taste		

Double-boiled bird's nest and pau sum ginseng

Regardless of its high price, this soup is still the doting mother's favourite brew for her brood. It is very *yurn*, which is a term the Cantonese use to describe a sense of "soothing" that works from inside-out and is thorough. The soup is also said to ensure the balanced functioning of the respiratory system, as well as improve the complexion.

Bird's nest	25 g, soaked, cleaned and drained	✧ Combine all ingredients in a double-boiler or heatproof (flameproof) dish. Double-boil for 4 hours.
Pau sum ginseng	20 g	✧ At the end of the cooking time, carefully remove cover of the dish or double-boiler, wipe clean of water droplets to prevent them from dripping into soup and replace. Serve hot or cold.
Water	2¹/₂ l (6 bowls)	
Rock sugar	150 g	

Chicken with cordyceps

Serves 4–6

This has been a favourite brew of caring mothers. Cordyceps rate high in promoting the well-being of young and old, healthy and ailing.

Chicken	1, about 1 kg	✧ Clean chicken. Discard head, neck and legs. Skin, then cut into large pieces.
Cordyceps *(dong chong xia cao / tung chung cho)*	30 g	✧ Combine all ingredients in a saucepan. Simmer for 3–4 hours. Serve hot.
Salt	¹/₂ tsp	
Water	2 l (8 bowls)	

Sweet Brews

Sugar cane and water chestnut tea
Serves 4–6

This is a very *yurn* or "soothing" tea and is preferred to cooling teas that are unsuitable for children whose constitutions are not strong enough for cooling foods. Cogongrass root can be found in most wet markets, as can stalks of sugar cane. If your child's constitution tends to be *yin* or inclined towards coolness, omit cogongrass root.

Sugar cane	600 g, washed and cut into 10-cm lengths	✧ Combine all ingredients in a saucepan. Simmer for up to 3 hours. Drink warm.
Cogongrass root (*bai mau gen / maw gun*)	100 g	
Sugared winter melon strips	100 g	
Water chestnuts	20–25, peeled	
Water	2 l (8 bowls)	

Pearl barley water
Serves 4–6

This is usually given on hot days to combat feverish conditions and cool a potentially overheating body. More importantly, it relieves diarrhoea, aids in urination, alleviates indigestion and promotes appetite.

Pearl barley	50 g, washed and drained	✧ Combine barley, winter melon strips and water in a pot. Bring to the boil and sustain for 45 minutes. Add sugar. Boil for 15–20 minutes more. Drink warm.
Sugared winter melon strips	12–15 pieces	
Water	2½ l (10 bowls)	
Rock sugar	100 g	

Lotus seeds, longan, Solomon's seal and barley
Serves 4–6

This is a sweet herbal brew that is deliciously quenching whether served hot or cold.

Precooked lotus seeds	50	✧ Except for rock sugar, combine all other ingredients in a large saucepan. Simmer over low heat for 45 minutes. Add sugar, adjust sweetness to taste if necessary. Simmer 10 minutes more. Remove from heat. Serve.
Dried longan flesh	75 g, washed and drained	
Solomon's seal (*yu zhu / yok chok*)	50 g	
Barley	50 g, washed and drained	
Water	2 l (8 bowls)	
Rock sugar	150 g	

Soybean milk

Serves 4–6

The nutritional value of this delicious drink is without question. Castor, brown or cane sugar can be used in this recipe, but keep the sugar level low.

Soy beans	500 g, soaked in water overnight
Water	3 l (12 bowls)
Sugar	200 g
Salt	1 pinch
Screwpine (*pandan*) leaves	3, washed and knotted

Tips
- It is important to ensure that the soybean milk is well boiled or else there will be a strong 'beany' smell. If using brown or cane sugar, adjust to taste as these impart less sweetness than the same amount of castor (superfine) sugar. Liquid amount is equally adjustable as some like their soybean milk thicker than others.
- Some older folk prefer to substitute honey for sugar as the latter tends to encourage phlegm in the throat. If you prefer honey, cook as above without any sugar, then add honey just before drinking warm.
- For added nutrition, crack 1 raw egg into a serving bowl, beat lightly, then add boiling soybean milk, stir and serve.

- Combine beans and water in a blender (processor). After blending well, strain with muslin bag for soybean milk.
- Transfer soybean milk to a large saucepan. Add sugar, salt and screwpine leaves. Bring to the boil over low heat. Simmer for 30 minutes. Stir occasionally.
- When done, remove from heat. Leave to cool, then strain. Serve hot or cold.

Buddha's fruit with winter melon

Serves 4–6

This is a popular sweet brew drunk to soothe and cool the body. Both red dates and longan impart sweetness, so adding rock sugar is optional.

Winter melon	1, medium-size
Buddha's fruit (*luo han guo* / *lor hawn gor*)	1
Dried red dates (*hong zao* / *hung cho*)	20, stones removed
Dried longan flesh	100 g, washed and drained
Water	2$\frac{1}{2}$ l (10 bowls)
Sugar (optional)	100 g

- Cut winter melon into quarters. Peel skin, seed and cut into 1-cm thick strips.
- Combine all ingredients in a pot. Simmer over low heat for 1–2 hours. Drink warm.

Tip
- If you find winter melon too much work to prepare, you can omit it and just combine Buddha's fruit, red dates and dried longan.

Double-boiled eggs with red dates
Serves 4–6

This recipe makes a nutritious brew that is a favourite with children. The sugar level here is kept low as the red dates already impart sweetness to the brew.

Dried red dates (*hong zao / hung cho*)	20, stones removed
Fresh eggs	6, well washed
Water	1¹/₂ l (6 bowls)
Rock sugar	100 g

Tip
* If you are in a hurry, boil instead of double-boiling eggs.

◇ Combine all ingredients in a double-boiler or heatproof (flameproof) bowl. Double-boil for 20 minutes or until eggs are cooked. Remove eggs and leave to cool. Shell cooled eggs.
◇ Return shelled eggs to brew. Double-boil for 3–4 hours. Before serving, drain and squeeze dates for liquid to return to brew. Discard pulp. Serve hot in individual bowls, one egg per person.

Quail's eggs with red dates
Serves 4–6

A delightful sweet brew that is both nourishing and nutritive, especially for growing children.

Quail's eggs	20, well washed, hard-boiled and shelled
Dried red dates (*hong zao / hung cho*)	40, stones removed
Water	2 l (8 bowls)

◇ Combine all ingredients in a pot. Simmer for 2–3 hours. Before serving, drain and squeeze dates for liquid to return to brew. Discard pulp. Serve warm.

Tip
* If you find that the brew is not sweet enough, add about 100 g rock sugar and bring to the boil. Then, remove from heat and serve.

Five treasures brew
Serves 4–6

A very heartening and satisfying brew — the longan adds sweetness, the quail's egg gives fullness, while the persimmon adds a crunchy note.

Dried persimmons	5 discs
Quail's eggs	12–15, hard-boiled and shelled
Agar-agar	25 g, soaked to soften and drained
Precooked lotus seeds	50
Dried longan flesh	100 g, washed and drained
Water	2–2¹/₂ l (8–10 bowls)
Rock sugar	100 g

◇ Soak dried persimmons in warm water for 5–10 minutes. Wash off powdery coating. Remove hard cores. Cut remaining parts into thin slivers. Set aside.
◇ Except for rock sugar and persimmon, combine all other ingredients in a saucepan. Boil for 30 minutes.
◇ Add remaining ingredients. Boil 10–15 minutes more. Remove from heat. Serve hot.

ADOLESCENCE TO ADULTHOOD

The adolescent years have their share of stress, strain and emotional ups and downs. Along with the physical changes that come with puberty, adolescents also have to cope with often invisible but very real growing pains. During this time, listlessness, poor appetite and low energy levels can take their toll.

For girls, the onset of menstruation also introduces discomforts such as abdominal cramps and spasms, irregular periods, excessive flow and premenstrual tension. Mothers with daughters should closely monitor their young charges for severe menstrual cramps or difficult periods.These adverse conditions can aggravate what is already a difficult and awkward stage in their lives.

Asian girls generally learn from a young age certain commonsense rules about keeping healthy. They are advised to wrap up well to keep out coldness, dampness and wind — this includes not going to bed with wet hair. Since abdominal cramps are believed to be caused by internal coldness, mothers teach their daughters that cooling or *yin* foods, which lead to congestion of the veins, are not to be consumed when they are having their periods. These include iced or cold drinks, cabbage, celery, broccoli, radishes, bananas, grapefruit and peas, as well as all sharp, sour-tasting foods and juices.

Girls are also taught that the adverse effects of chills and colds, which lead to poor circulation, cold feet and menstrual cramps, can be prevented or countered with quick, hot baths and warming brews. The rationale behind this advice is based on sound commonsense. Hot baths tone up the system and improve circulation, and loss of blood is followed by loss of energy, which explains the many invigorating, stimulating soups using black beans, liver and chicken with Chinese angelica (*dang gui / dong kwai*) advocated to help the body repair itself. These are sure-fire ways to combat low energy levels, as well as ease abdominal cramps and pains.

Mothers of adolescent boys growing into manhood should likewise closely monitor their diet to ensure sufficient reserves of energy for the near-endless list of activities they participate in, from school studies to examinations and extracurricular activities. Deficiencies in their diet will not only cause ill health, but also retard growth.

The dietary needs of adulthood are only slightly different from those of the earlier years. The physical and mental energy used up on a daily basis must be restored or the body will succumb to a host of common ills. Differences arise only with regard to the types of ingredients considered suitable for one age group and not another. Without a proper diet, the body's resistance lowers and will be unable to combat even common infections like coughs and colds.

Although the adult male does not experience the same physiological discomforts of the female, a poor diet of junk food, fast food and hawker fare, together with habits of drinking and/or smoking will, in the long term, result in considerable nutritional deficiencies and their corresponding health problems. Some effective and tasty ways of fighting fatigue, combating stresses of different kinds and increasing energy levels include drinking teas concocted from chrysanthemum and boxthorn fruit (*gou qi zi / gei chi*) and nourishing soups and brews, especially those cooked with chicken and dates.

Female adults who suffer from intense menstrual cramps will find much relief from Chinese angelica (*dang gui / dong kwai*) — a root that is both astringent and heating. In imparting warmth, Chinese angelica stimulates blood circulation, builds and nourishes the female organs and relieves amenorrhoea (stoppage of normal monthly periods or scanty periods). Other herbs the adult woman should use in her diet are ginger, ginseng, Chinese teas, dates, boxthorn fruit and Chinese yam (*shan yao / wai san*). These can be cooked in innumerable ways to promote health and prevent anaemia.

Recipes

Main meals

Soups and porridges:
1. Chinese radish with dried cuttlefish soup p.100
2. Marrow soup p.100
3. Black bean and pork rib soup p.101
4. Herbal poultry soup p.101
5. *Yeh hiong fa* and liver soup p.102
6. White fungus and chicken p.102
7. Frog's leg porridge p.104
8. *Bak kut teh* (Herbal pork rib soup) p.105
9. Eight treasures soup p.106

Dishes:
1. Steamed chicken with ginger p.108
2. Stir-fried beef with ginger and spring onions p.108
3. Savoury tripe p.109
4. Stir-fried health platter p.110
5. Stir-fried anchovies with celery p.110
6. Fried anchovies with peanuts p.111
7. Trotter with Chinese radish and ginger p.112
8. Stewed trotter with lotus root p.112
9. Chicken with longan and dates p.114
10. Fried frog's legs in ginger and spring onions p.114

Sweets and Brews

Sweets:
1. Double-boiled bird's nest with coconut milk p.116
2. Steamed winter melon p.117
5. Sweet potato, yam and sago porridge p.117
3. Red bean porridge p.118
4. *Ma thai loh* (Water chestnut cream) p.118

Curative teas:
1. Ginger tea p.120
2. Boxthorn fruit tea p.120
3. Sweet marrow tea p.121
4. *Pau sum* ginseng tea p.121
5. Chrysanthemum tea p.121
6. Eight herbs tea p.122
7. Codonopsis, astragalus, black and red date tea p.122
8. Codonopsis, boxthorn fruit, longan and red date tea p.124

Tonic brews:
1. *Fatt thieu cheong* (Buddha jumps over the wall) p.125
3. Chinese angelica and donkey's glue p.126
2. Double-boiled chicken with Chinese angelica p.126

Soups and porridges

Chinese radish with dried cuttlefish soup
Serves 4–6

Chinese radish is believed to be a detoxifying agent and some Chinese households faithfully serve this soup at least once fortnightly to neutralise any toxic or poisonous matter in the body. In the same vein, any dish cooked with radish should not to be eaten when one is also consuming a herbal prescription as all the nutritive properties will be similarly neutralised. It is said that people who suffer the uncomfortable and congested effects of overeating potent or rich foods such as ginseng can get near-immediate relief by swallowing a spoonful or two of Chinese radish juice.

Chinese radishes	2, medium-size; scraped and cut into 3-cm cubes
Dried cuttlefish	3 pieces
Pork ribs or beef bones	300 g, cut into smaller pieces
Dried red dates (*hong zao / hung cho*)	6, stones removed
Dried oysters	6, cleaned and soaked
Ginger	3-cm knob, crushed
Water	2 l (8 bowls)
Salt	1/2 tsp or more to taste
Pepper to taste	

✧ Remove eyes of cuttlefish. Cut tentacles into two lengthways (lengthwise). Cut each of the remaining pieces into four. Soak in water for 5 minutes. Drain and clean off grit before cooking.

✧ Except for radishes and pepper, combine all other ingredients in a saucepan. Boil over moderate heat for 30 minutes. Add radishes and pepper. Cook for 20 minutes more. Add water if evaporation has been intense. Serve hot.

Marrow soup
Serves 4–6

Known in Cantonese as *lo wong kwa*, or "old cucumber", the coarse- and brown-skinned marrow is reputed for its cleansing and purifying properties.

Pork ribs	500 g, cut into smaller pieces
Marrow	1, medium-size; seeded and cut into rings
Stock	1 1/2 l (6 bowls)
Dried scallops	6, soaked
Salt	1/2 tsp or more to taste
Pepper to taste	
Spring onion (scallion)	1 stalk, chopped

✧ Except for pepper and spring onion, combine all other ingredients in a pot. Simmer over low heat for 1–1 1/2 hours. Add pepper to taste. Garnish with spring onions. Serve hot.

Black bean and pork rib soup
Serves 4–6

This simple soup is an invaluable tonic for both young and old. Believed to clear skin ailments, it is also excellent for menstruating women. This is because it builds and blood and hence, helps to replace lost blood.

Black beans	200 g, toasted in a dry nonstick pan until jumping, then swirled under a running tap and drained
Pork ribs	250 g, cut into smaller pieces
Old ginger	3-cm knob, sliced
Dried oysters	8–10, cleaned and soaked
Water	2 l (8 bowls)
Salt	$\frac{1}{2}$ tsp or more to taste

✧ Combine all ingredients in a large saucepan. Simmer for 2–3 hours. Drink soup warm. Both black beans and pork ribs can be eaten, but some people focus only on the soup.

Herbal poultry soup
Serves 4–6

This is a nutritious and lip-smacking dish. If preferred, use 10 quail's eggs instead of four chicken's eggs.

Chicken	500 g, cut into large pieces
Duck	500 g, cut into large pieces
Eggs	4, hard-boiled and shelled
Dried black dates (*hei zao / hak cho*)	20, stones removed
Boxthorn fruit (*gou qi zi / gei chi*)	2 heaped Tbsp, washed and drained
Codonopsis root (*dang shen / dong sum*)	20 g
Cnidium root (*chuan xiong / chuen kung*)	15 g
Water	2–2$\frac{1}{2}$ l (8–10 bowls)
Salt	$\frac{1}{2}$ tsp or more to taste

✧ Combine all ingredients in a large saucepan. Simmer over low heat for 3–4 hours. Serve hot.

Tip
✧ If you like your soup free of oil or fat, remove skin, fat and gristle from poultry before cooking. Alternatively, skim fatty layer from surface before serving.

Yeh hiong fa and liver soup

Serves 4–6

Inexpensive and not strictly a herb, *yeh hiong fa* literally translates into "flower of night fragrance" in Cantonese and is sold as a vegetable in most wet markets. It has little buds and is reputedly good for one's eyesight.

Water	1 l (4 bowls)	
Yeh hiong fa	250 g, washed and cut into smaller pieces	
Liver	150 g, cut into smaller pieces	
Salt	½ tsp	
Pepper to taste		

✧ Bring water to the boil in a saucepan. Add *yeh hiong fah*. Stir once, then add liver pieces. Add salt and pepper to taste. Remove and serve hot.

White fungus and chicken

Serves 4–6

White fungus has a crunchy, elastic texture that does not endear it to many people. As a curative food, however, it is known for rendering a smooth complexion to those who take it regularly. Use very little in cooking as it swells up to 12 times its original size when cooked.

Dried white fungus (*bai mu er / shuet yi*)	25 g
Chicken	1, about 1½ kg
Water	2 l (8 bowls)
Salt	½ tsp or more to taste

✧ Soak fungus in hot water for 30–45 minutes. Remove dirt and clean well with several changes of water. Squeeze out all water. Separate clumps into smaller pieces.
✧ Clean chicken. Discard head, neck, legs and gristle. Trim off excess fat. Skin, then cut into large pieces.
✧ Except for fungus, combine all other ingredients in a large saucepan. Simmer over low heat for 20 minutes. Add fungus. Simmer for 30 minutes more. Serve hot.

Frog's leg porridge
Serves 4–6

This is gourmet fare that also doubles up as a reliable cure for appetite loss in children.
For practical purposes and convenience, the frog's legs in this recipe are cooked altogether
instead of in batches for individual serves.

Rice	250 g, washed and drained
Water	1½ l (6 bowls)
Salt	½ tsp or more to taste
Frog's legs	10–12
Ginger juice	extracted from 4-cm knob
Light soy sauce	2 Tbsp
Sesame seed oil	1 Tbsp
Century eggs	6, shelled, washed and cut into wedges
Crisp-fried shallots	4 Tbsp
Young ginger	4-cm knob, shredded
Spring onions (scallions)	3 stalks, finely chopped

⬦ Soak rice in water and salt for 15 minutes. Set aside.

⬦ Season frog's legs with ginger juice, soy sauce and sesame seed oil. Leave for 15 minutes.

⬦ Boil rice for 20 minutes. When rice grains break, adjust liquid amount to suit your preference. Then, bring porridge to an intense boil. Add seasoned frog's legs. Stir carefully and well for 10–15 minutes or until frog's legs are cooked through.

⬦ To serve, put a few wedges of century eggs into a bowl before adding porridge over the top. Garnish with shallot slices, ginger and spring onions, as well as a dribble of sesame seed oil if desired.

Tips

❖ Cooking this dish restaurant or hawker-style is tedious and time-consuming — the frog's legs are cooked only just before someone wants to eat it and only 1 serve at a time. If preferred, bring the porridge to an intense boil, then add enough frog's legs for 1 person and boil for 10–15 minutes. Scoop out frog's legs and sufficient porridge to serve. Repeat the process for each serving. Garnish as above.

❖ Century eggs are preserved duck's eggs that have been buried with earth, lime and straw inside urns for up to 2 months. Shelled century eggs are dark-coloured; what used to be the egg white is black and the yolk is a greenish-grey. The eggs have a pungent odour and are savoury in taste. They are considered a delicacy and eaten as *hors d'oeuvres* with pickled ginger slices.

Bak kut teh (Herbal pork rib soup)
Serves 4–6

Traditional hawker fare, this dish has since become a household favourite and is actually a rich and nourishing brew that boasts of tonic herbs. Your neighbourhood herbalist will be able to make the appropriate blend for *bak kut teh* if you tell him or her how much meat you intend to use. You can also buy prepacked *bak kut teh* blends in supermarkets. Of late, other meats such as chicken have been used instead of pork in this brew.

Water	3 l (12 bowls)
Pork tenderloin	500 g, cut into two
Pork ribs	500 g, cut into smaller pieces
Light soy sauce	3 Tbsp
Dark soy sauce	1 Tbsp
Salt	1/2 tsp or more to taste
Star anise	1, finely pounded
Cinnamon stick	2-cm length, broken into segments
Garlic	10–12 cloves, crushed
Chinese angelica (*dang gui / dong kwai*)	60 g
Boxthorn fruit (*gou qi zi / gei chi*)	3 Tbsp
Sugar cane	2 10-cm lengths
Deep-fried soybean puffs (*taufu pok*)	12, small; halved
Pepper to taste	

Garnish:

Coriander (cilantro) leaves	1 sprig, chopped
Deep-fried dough sticks (*you tiao / yau chow kwai*)	12, cut into 2-cm lengths

Dipping sauce:

Red chillies	5, finely sliced
Light soy sauce	3–4 Tbsp

✧ Bring water to the boil in a large saucepan. Except for soybean puffs and pepper, add all other ingredients. Bring to another boil. Simmer over low heat for 1 hour or until meat is tender.

✧ Add soybean puffs. Cook for 10 minutes more. Remove tenderloin pieces, cut into bite-size pieces and return to soup. Heat for 5 minutes. Add pepper to taste.

✧ To serve, garnish with coriander leaves, then add dough stick pieces. Eat meat with chilli slices in light soy sauce on the side.

Eight treasures soup

Serves 4–6

Canned bamboo shoots	1 can, drained and sliced
Canned button mushrooms	1/2 can, drained
Dried Chinese mushrooms	12, soaked and sliced
Dried black dates (*hei zao / hak cho*)	15–20, stones removed
Boxthorn fruit (*gou qi zi / gei chi*)	3 Tbsp
Chinese angelica (*dang gui / dong kwai*)	30 g
Cnidium root (*chuan xiong / chuen kung*)	50 g
Boxthorn leaves (*gou qi cai / gau gei choy*)	30 g
Water	1 1/2 l (6 bowls)
Salt	1/2 tsp or more to taste
Chinese cooking wine (*hua tiao / fa dew*)	2 Tbsp
Sesame seed oil	1 tsp

✧ Except for wine and sesame seed oil, combine all other ingredients in a double-boiler. Double-boil for 1–1 1/2 hours.

✧ Bring to the boil by increasing heat, then add wine. Remove and serve with sesame seed oil.

Steamed chicken with ginger
Serves 4–6

Ginger is often used to treat suppressed menstruation. It is *yang* in energy and therefore invaluable in combating ailments caused by internal or external coldness.

Chicken	1, about 1 kg; replaceable with 3 chicken thighs
Young ginger	300 g, peeled and grated
Pepper	1/2 tsp
Salt	1/2 tsp or more to taste
Rice wine	2 Tbsp
Sesame seed oil	1 Tbsp
Dried Chinese mushrooms	3, soaked, stems removed and finely sliced
Spring onions (scallions)	2 stalks, finely chopped

◇ Clean chicken. Discard head, neck and legs. Skin, then cut into average-size pieces.

◇ Season chicken with ginger, pepper, salt, wine and sesame seed oil. Leave for 20 minutes.

◇ Combine chicken and mushrooms in a heatproof (flameproof) dish. Steam for 30 minutes or until meat is cooked. Serve hot. Garnish with spring onions.

Stir-fried beef with ginger and spring onions
Serves 4–6

Beef helps to alleviate anaemia and this is a popular and delicious way of preparing stir-fried beef.

Lean beef (rump or steak)	400 g, finely sliced
Chinese cooking wine (*hua tiao / fa dew*)	2 Tbsp
Cornflour (cornstarch)	1/2 Tbsp
Cooking oil	3 Tbsp
Ginger	2 4-cm knobs, finely sliced
Garlic	2 cloves, crushed
Dark soy sauce	2 Tbsp
Sugar	1/2 tsp or more to taste
Spring onions (scallions)	12 stalks, cut into 5-cm lengths
Salt	1/2 tsp or more to taste
Red chillies	3, finely sliced

◇ Season beef with wine for 10–15 minutes. Mix in cornflour.

◇ Heat oil in a wok. Add ginger and garlic. Stir-fry for 1 minute. Add beef. Stir-fry for 2 minutes. Add soy sauce and sugar. Stir-fry a while. Add spring onions and salt. Stir-fry until meat is tender. Add 1–2 Tbsp water if necessary.

◇ To serve, garnish with sliced red chillies. Alternatively, add chillies last to the wok, stir a couple of times, then dish out. Eat hot.

Tip

❖ To tenderise any meat, wrap in unripe papaya slices or very young papaya leaves. For 500 g meat, leave to tenderise for 30–45 minutes. If using papaya leaves, wash well and crush a little before wrapping.

Savoury tripe
Serves 4–6

Many Chinese subscribe to the theory of organotherapy, which suggests that consuming pig's tripe will nourish the human stomach.

Pig's tripe	1, thoroughly cleaned
Dried Chinese mushroom stalks	20, soaked
Water	1 ½ l (6 bowls)
Peppercorns (optional)	10–15, crushed
Gingko nuts (*bai guo / bak gor*)	20, shelled
Water chestnuts	12, washed and peeled
Salt to taste	
Dried bean curd sticks (*fu zhu / fu chok*)	4, broken into 3-cm lengths and soaked in water
Abalone (optional)	1 can, thinly sliced

⬧ Except for bean curd sticks and abalone, combine all other ingredients in a pot. Cover and simmer for 1–1¼ hours.

⬧ Add bean curd sticks. Cook for 30 minutes. Add abalone. Cook for 5 minutes more. Serve hot.

Tip

❖ Tripe or any type of offal has to be cleaned thoroughly before cooking. Some wet markets and supermarkets sell cleaned offal. Should you need to clean tripe at home, rinse under running water before rubbing with tamarind pulp to remove the slime. Rinse with water, then rub with sago or tapioca flour or cornstarch. Rinse again with water and lastly, rub with plenty of salt to remove remaining traces of slime. When done, turn inside out and scrape with a knife. This helps to remove any unpleasant odours, which will be later masked by the addition of peppercorns during cooking. Wash tripe one last time with vinegar and salt and drain well. Heat a dry wok until very hot. Singe well by turning from side to side several times. Remove and wash again under running water.

Stir-fried health platter
Serves 4–6

This vegetable dish has both crunch and goodness.

Cooking oil	4 Tbsp
Pork loin	200 g, finely sliced
Canned bamboo shoots	100 g
Skinned roasted peanuts (groundnuts)	80 g
Shelled prawns (shrimps)	300 g
Soft bean curd	3 pieces, quartered
Diced cucumber	100 g
Green peas	100 g
Carrots	100 g, cut into 2-cm lengths

Sauce:

Cornstarch (cornflour)	1 tsp
Water	1 Tbsp
Light soy sauce	1 Tbsp
Sugar	1/2 tsp
Soybean paste (dou jiang / dau cheong)	1 Tbsp

✧ Heat 3 Tbsp oil in wok Stir-fry pork until colour has changed. Add remaining ingredients. Stir-fry for 5 minutes. Remove from wok and set aside.

✧ Combine all sauce ingredients in a bowl. Heat remaining oil in wok. When hot, add sauce mixture. Stir-fry until fragrant and bubbling. Add cooked ingredients and stir to mix well for 5–8 minutes. Serve warm.

Stir-fried anchovies with celery
Serves 4–6

If you like crunch and crispiness, this flavourful and nutritious dish will appeal to your palate. It can be eaten by itself or as a side dish with noodles or rice. Celery contains a fair amount of vitamins and minerals, while anchovies are rich in calcium.

Cooking oil	3 Tbsp
Ginger	2-cm knob, shredded
Onion	1, large; sliced
Anchovies	100 g, washed and dried
Celery sticks	2, thickly sliced
Rice wine	2 Tbsp
Salt (optional)	1/2 tsp
Pepper to taste	

✧ Heat oil in a wok. Add ginger and onion. Fry until fragrant. Add anchovies and fry until crispy. Add celery. Fry for 30 seconds. Add wine, salt and pepper. Stir-fry a few times until liquid dries up. Serve hot.

Fried anchovies with peanuts
Serves 4–6

This delicious dish is great for whetting an appetite and is usually served as
a side dish with rice.

Raw shelled peanuts (groundnuts)	100 g, grit or sand removed
Anchovies	200 g
Cooking oil	125 ml (1/2 bowl)
Onions	2, large
Red chillies	3–4
Sugar	1 tsp

✧ Toast peanuts in a dry wok over very low heat until cooked through, stirring continuously. The skins would have broken up after toasting. Remove to a flat container and while rotating it, blow gently to remove skins. Alternatively, place in a cloth and rub off skins.

✧ To clean dried, salted anchovies, remove heads and backbones. Soak in water for a few minutes. Drain well. Leave to dry in the sun for at least 1 hour. Alternatively, air in a dry place after using kitchen paper to absorb excess water.

✧ Heat oil in a wok. Fry anchovies until crispy. Anchovies tend to absorb a lot of oil, so add more oil if necessary or if you like an oilier dish. Drain anchovies and set aside. Reserve remaining oil in wok.

✧ Grind (process) onion, chillies and sugar. Fry ground mixture in reserved oil until fragrant. Add anchovies. Stir-fry for 5–8 minutes, turning well. Add peanuts. Stir well to mix.

Trotter with Chinese radish and ginger

Serves 4–6

This version of trotter includes Chinese radish and is not cooked for mothers in confinement as radish is considered too *yin* or cooling for them.

Pig's trotter (foreleg)	1, about 1 1/2 kg
Cooking oil	3 Tbsp; replaceable with sesame seed oil
Garlic	3 cloves, crushed
Young ginger	300 g, pounded once and cut into chunks
Chinese radishes	2, medium-size, about 600 g; peeled and cut into chunks
Water	250 ml (1 bowl)
Palm sugar (*gula melaka*)	1 whole piece, softened with hot water and sieved
Black vinegar	250 ml (1 bowl)
Salt to taste	

◇ Cut trotter into average-size pieces. Blanch in boiling water for 10 minutes. Rinse off grease.

◇ Heat oil in a wok. Add garlic and ginger. Fry for 1 minute. Add trotter. Stir for 10 minutes. Add radishes. Stir-fry a while. Transfer to a clay pot.

◇ Add sufficient water to cover ingredients. Bring to the boil. Simmer for 30 minutes. Add palm sugar, vinegar and salt. Simmer for 15 minutes or until meat texture is to your taste. Stir occasionally to ensure meat does not stick to pot. Add liquid if necessary.

Stewed trotter with lotus root

Serves 4–6

Pig's trotter (foreleg)	1, about 1 kg
Cooking oil	4 Tbsp
Ginger	4-cm knob, crushed and sliced
Red fermented bean curd (*nan ru* / *nam yue*)	3 pieces, well mashed
Garlic	4 cloves, diced
Rice wine	2 Tbsp
Sugar	2 Tbsp
Dark soy sauce	1 Tbsp
Light soy sauce	1 Tbsp
Water	1 1/2 l (6 bowls)
Lotus root	300 g, skin scrapped off and cut into rings
Salt	1/2 tsp or more to taste
Spring onions (scallions)	3 stalks, finely chopped

◇ Cut trotter into large pieces. Blanch in boiling water for 10 minutes. Rinse off grease.

◇ Heat 2 Tbsp oil in wok. Fry ginger, as well as half the fermented bean curd and garlic. Add trotter. Stir well for 5 minutes. Add wine, sugar, soy sauces and water. Stir a few times. Transfer to a clay pot. Cover and leave to simmer.

◇ Heat remaining oil in wok. Fry remaining fermented bean curd and garlic. Add lotus root. Cook for 5 minutes. Add to clay pot. Add salt. Simmer for 45 minutes or until soft and cooked through.

◇ To serve, garnish with spring onions.

Chicken with longan and dates

Serves 4–6

Chicken	1, about 1–1¹/₂ kg; trimmed of excess fat and cut into large pieces
Ginger	4-cm knob, finely sliced
Rice wine	4 Tbsp
Light soy sauce	1 Tbsp
Dark soy sauce	1 Tbsp
Salt	¹/₂ tsp
Sugar	¹/₂ tsp
Spring onions (scallions)	2 stalks, chopped

Marinade:

Water	500 ml (2 bowls)
Dried red dates (*hong zao / hung cho*)	8, stones removed
Dried black dates (*hei zao / hak cho*)	8, stones removed
Dried longan flesh	25 g
Celery	100 g, cut into 3-cm lengths

✧ Combine marinade ingredients in a large bowl. Marinate chicken for 45–60 minutes. Transfer to a clay pot.

✧ Except for spring onions, add remaining ingredients. Simmer over low heat for 1–1¹/₂ hours. Check for liquid evaporation and add water if necessary. Serve hot. Garnish with spring onions.

Fried frog's legs in ginger and spring onions

Serves 4–6

This is a gourmet dish eaten to whet the appetite or as a side dish.
Omit Chinese cooking wine if serving to children and use a thick stock instead.

Frog's legs	8–10
Chinese cooking wine (*hua tiao / fa dew*)	2 Tbsp
Cornflour (cornstarch)	2 Tbsp
Salt	¹/₂ tsp
Sesame seed oil	1 Tbsp
Cooking oil	3 Tbsp
Ginger	4-cm knob, finely sliced
Light soy sauce	1 tsp or more to taste
Red chilli	1
Spring onions (scallions)	5 stalks, finely sliced
Pepper to taste	

✧ Season frog's legs with wine, cornflour, salt and sesame seed oil. Set aside for 15 minutes.

✧ Heat cooking oil in a wok. Fry ginger. Add frog's legs and stir-fry until nearly golden brown. Add soy sauce, chilli and spring onions. Fry over reduced heat for 5 minutes. Add pepper to taste.

✧ Serve hot and garnished with chilli slices and spring onions if desired.

Sweets

Double-boiled bird's nest with coconut milk
Serves 4–6

Bird's nest is extolled for its manifold properties. Parents pay a ransom for it to give to their children so that they will withstand colds and chills and have good circulatory systems — in short, to ensure their general good health. This recipe is an interesting and flavourful way of eating bird's nest as coconut milk adds an unusual touch.

Bird's nest	25 g, thoroughly cleaned
Precooked lotus seeds	30
Water	1 l (4 bowls)
Rock sugar	100 g
Thick coconut milk	250 ml (1 bowl), squeezed from 1 grated coconut and sufficient water

✧ Except for coconut milk, combine all other ingredients in a double-boiler or heatproof (flameproof) bowl. Double-boil for 4 hours.
✧ Bring coconut milk to the boil in a saucepan. Then, remove from heat immediately.
✧ To serve, spoon hot bird's nest into individual serving bowls. Top with spoonfuls of coconut milk.

Tip
❖ Do not add too much coconut milk to the bird's nest if serving to young children. The rich milk might overload or upset their digestive systems.
❖ Health conscious cooks can use low-fat coconut milk.

Steamed winter melon

Serves 4–6

This is a sweet that can be eaten any time of the day or to accompany a meal.

Winter melon	1, medium-size
Rock sugar	50 g
Dried red dates (*hong zao / hung cho*)	20, stones removed
Dried longan flesh	100 g
Water	2 Tbsp

✧ Slice off top of melon. Remove seeds. Scoop out a hole big enough for stuffing. Reserve melon flesh.

✧ Combine some melon flesh with remaining ingredients. Add water only if necessary.

✧ Pack combined ingredients into melon. Replace melon top. Use toothpicks or cocktail sticks to hold firmly in place.

✧ Sit whole melon in a deep heatproof (flameproof) bowl that fits such that melon will not wobble. Alternatively, slice off part of the melon's bottom before filling with ingredients. Steam over low heat for 1½–2 hours. Serve hot.

Sweet potato, yam and sago porridge

Serves 4–6

Sweet potatoes	250 g, peeled and cut into 2-cm cubes
Yam	250 g, peeled and cut into 2-cm cubes
Water	1½ l (6 bowls)
Thick coconut milk	375 ml (1½ bowls), squeezed from 1 grated coconut and sufficient water
Sugar	150 g
Salt	1 pinch
Screwpine (*pandan*) leaves	4, knotted in pairs
Sago	2 Tbsp, washed in cold water and drained

✧ Combine sweet potatoes, yam and water in a pot. Boil until soft.

✧ Add coconut milk, sugar, salt and screwpine leaves. Slowly bring to the boil. When mixture is boiling, add sago. Boil for 4–5 minutes more. Remove and serve.

Tip
❖ Health conscious cooks can use low-fat coconut milk.

Red bean porridge

Serves 4–6

Red adzuki beans	200 g, washed and drained
Salt (optional)	1/4 tsp
Precooked lotus seeds	25 g
Dried tangerine peel	3 pieces
Water	2 l (8 bowls)
Palm sugar (*gula melaka*)	1 whole piece
Sago	2 Tbsp, washed in cold water and drained
Sugar	100 g
Screwpine (*pandan*) leaves	4, knotted in pairs
Thick coconut milk	250 ml (1 bowl), squeezed from 1 grated coconut and sufficient water

◇ Combine red beans, salt, lotus seeds, tangerine peel and water in a saucepan. Simmer for 2–2½ hours or until beans expand or split.

◇ Add palm sugar, sago, sugar and screwpine leaves. Boil for 10–15 minutes more, stirring well until sugar has completely dissolved.

◇ Remove screwpine leaves. Serve with coconut milk.

Tips

❖ You can squeeze for a more diluted coconut milk, about 250–375 ml (1–1½ bowls), from the same grated coconut. If desired, add thin coconut milk to boiling beans last, then stir well for 5 minutes before removing from heat. Remember, however, to reduce liquid amount called for in the recipe accordingly. Cooked red beans will not stay fresh or store as long when coconut milk has been added. Health conscious cooks can use low-fat coconut milk.

❖ Beans and pulses cook faster if a porcelain spoon is added to the saucepan when boiling them.

Ma thai loh (Water chestnut cream)

Serves 4–6

This is a very soothing and delightful sweet.

Water chestnuts	30, peeled, washed and finely chopped
Water	1½ l (6 bowls)
Sugar	150 g
Egg whites	2, well whisked

◇ Except for egg whites, combine all other ingredients in a double-boiler or heatproof (flameproof) dish. Double-boil for 1–2 hours.

◇ Before removing from heat, pour in egg whites and stir well. Remove and serve.

Curative teas

Ginger tea
Serves 1

Females from adolescence onwards may experience suppressed, painful or irregular menstruation. This tea, prepared and drunk once or twice a week, gives much needed relief, as well as warmth when suffering from chills or colds. The tea must not be stored overnight.

Ginger	2 4-cm knobs, crushed and thickly sliced
Dried red dates (*hong zao / hung cho*)	6, stones removed
Water	375 ml (1$\frac{1}{2}$ bowls)

✧ Combine all ingredients in a pot. Simmer for about 1$\frac{1}{2}$ hours or until liquid is reduced. Drain and squeeze dates for liquid to return to brew. Discard pulp.

✧ Drain and discard ginger. Drink brew warm once or twice a day.

Tip

✧ If using a method of cooking where little or no evaporation takes place, eg using a slow cooker, reduce liquid by 125 ml ($\frac{1}{2}$ bowl).

Boxthorn fruit tea
Serves 1

The easiest way to imbibe the goodness of boxthorn fruit, known as a reliable remedy for a list of ills from poor eyesight to diabetes, is to drink this tea two to three times a week.

Boxthorn fruit (*gou qi zi / gei chi*)	2 heaped Tbsp
Boiling water	250 ml (1 bowl)

Tip

✧ For a more traditional approach, simmer boxthorn fruit for about 1–1$\frac{1}{2}$ hours over low charcoal heat. Use 4 times the amount of water specified in the recipe and double the quantity of boxthorn fruit. In this case, store the resulting brew in a flask and drink throughout the day in place of water.

✧ Put boxthorn fruit into a porcelain mug. Add boiling hot water. Cover and leave to immerse for 10–15 minutes. Drink tea warm 3–4 times a day. If desired, add fresh boiling water a couple more times for thinner brews.

Sweet marrow tea

Serves 4–6

While marrow soup is served during meal times, this sweet version is drunk as a warm tea
any time of the day.

Marrow	1, medium-size; peeled, seeded and cut into rings
Water	1¹/₂ l (6 bowls)
Dried red dates (*hong zao / hung cho*)	15–20, stones removed
Rock sugar	150 g

✧ Combine all ingredients in a saucepan. Simmer for 2–3 hours.
✧ Drain and squeeze dates for liquid to return to brew. Discard pulp. Drink brew once or twice a day.

Pau sum ginseng tea

Serves 4–6

Pau sum ginseng is recommended to older children and adults to alleviate anaemia
and weaknesses such as breathlessness and lethargy as it promotes blood circulation.
It also relieves tension, headaches and eyestrain.

Pau sum ginseng	30 g
Water	2 l (8 bowls)

✧ Combine ingredients in a double-boiler or heatproof (flameproof) bowl. Double-boil for 4 hours.
✧ Alternatively, combine ingredients in a saucepan, with 125 ml (¹/₂ bowl) more water. Simmer over low heat for 3 hours. Leave to cool and stand overnight, although not in the refrigerator. Drink in the morning before leaving for work or school.

Chrysanthemum tea

Serves 4–6

Consumed weekly or fortnightly, this fragrant tea clears digestive upsets from oily food
or overeating and relieves internal heat.

Dried chrysanthemum flowers	30 g
Pau sum ginseng	30 g
Cordyceps (*dong chong xia cao / tung chung cho*)	30 g
Water	2 l (8 bowls)
Rock sugar	150 g

✧ Combine all ingredients in a saucepan. Simmer for 1 hour. Strain or leave to settle before drinking, warm or cold.

Tip
✧ For babies or toddlers, prepare chrysanthemum tea by putting 4–5 flowers and 85 ml (¹/₃ bowl) of water into a small porcelain bowl and steaming for 30 minutes. Add honey to taste and feed baby in small amounts — 1–2 tsp, 2–3 times a day, at intervals of 1–2 hours.

Eight herbs tea

Serves 2

This thick, slightly bitter tea is usually drunk at the end of the monthly menstruation to strengthen and restore energy. Some women take it once fortnightly. The brew is made from a blend of eight herbs — one of which is Chinese angelica (*dang gui / dong kwai*), which builds blood and nourishes the female glands — and can only be obtained from the herbalist. Shelled, hard-boiled eggs, lean pork or chicken and red dates are usually added to sweeten an otherwise unpalatable brew. This recipe, in serving two, is ideal for a mother and her teenage daughter. If you can stomach a thicker brew, reduce liquid by 125 mililitres, or one bowl, and use only one egg for one serve.

Eggs	2; replaceable with 1 chicken thigh or 200 g lean pork
Eight herbs tea	1 prescription
Water	375 ml (3 bowls)
Dried red dates (*hong zao / hung cho*)	10–12, stones removed

- ✧ If using eggs, hard-boil and shell them. If using chicken thigh, skin it. If using lean pork, include whole.
- ✧ Combine all ingredients in a clay pot. Bring to the boil. Simmer for 3–4 hours. Cover the clay pot spout with some tin foil to reduce evaporation. You should obtain about 500 ml (2 bowls) liquid. Drink warm before going to bed.

Codonopsis, astragalus, black and red date tea

Serves 4–6

This is a deceptively simple, sweetish tea that is excellent for the lungs and blood circulation. It is reputed to pep up the energy of the weak, undernourished or overworked and is good for anyone under stress or strain, eg students mugging for examinations. If climbing stairs is a challenge for you, try drinking this brew weekly for a couple of months.

Codonopsis root (*dang shen / dong sum*)	30 g
Astragalus root (*huang qi / puk kei*)	30 g
Dried red dates (*hong zao / hung cho*)	20, stones removed
Dried black dates (*hei zao / hak cho*)	20, stones removed
Water	2$\frac{1}{2}$ l (10 bowls)

- ✧ Combine all ingredients in a large saucepan. Bring to the boil. Simmer over low heat for 3–4 hours or until liquid is reduced to $^3/_4$ of original amount. Sip it warm.

Codonopsis, boxthorn fruit, longan and red date tea

Serves 4–6

This is a sweeter version of the previous brew because of the addition of boxthorn fruit and longan. Nonetheless, it has the same rejuvenating effect.

Codonopsis root (*dang shen / dong sum*)	30 g
Boxthorn fruit (*gou qi zi / gei chi*)	3 heaped Tbsp, washed and drained
Dried red dates (*hong zao / hung cho*)	30, stones removed
Dried longan flesh	100 g, washed and drained
Water	2^1/$_2$ l (10 bowls)

✧ Combine all ingredients in a large saucepan. Bring to the boil. Simmer for 3–4 hours or until liquid is reduced to ^{3}/$_4$ of original amount. Drink it warm.

Tonic brews

Fatt thieu cheong
(Buddha jumps over the wall)

The tonic efficacy of this delicious, flavourful and expensive dish is legendary, especially in building libido and fortifying energy. It is not unusual for restaurants to charge in excess of $1,000 for this speciality, which is usually served with rice noodles.

Pig's tripe	1, thoroughly cleaned (refer to p. 109)
Dried scallops	6, soaked and drained
Fish maw	6 pieces, soaked and drained
Chicken	6 pieces, meaty and average-size
Dried Chinese mushrooms	6, soaked and drained
Dried oysters	24, soaked and drained
Dried longan flesh	100g, washed and drained
Chinese yam (*shan yao / wai san*)	30 g
Chinese angelica (*dang gui / dong kwai*)	30 g
Astragalus root (*huang qi / puk kei*)	30 g
Codonopsis root (*dang shen / dong sum*)	30 g
Dried red dates (*hong zao / hung cho*)	25, stones removed
Chinese cooking wine (*hua tiao / fa dew*)	4 Tbsp
Shark's fin	150 g, soaked
Sea cucumbers	6, thoroughly cleaned
Canned abalone	6 slices
Salt and pepper to taste	

◇ Combine tripe, scallops, fish maw, chicken, mushrooms, oysters, longan, Chinese yam and angelica, astragalus and codonopsis roots and dates. Double-boil for 4 hours.

◇ Add wine, shark's fin, sea cucumbers and abalone. Double-boil for 10–15 minutes more. Add salt and pepper to taste. Serve hot.

Tips

❖ The traditional way of double-boiling this special soup is in an expensive, specially designed pot. If you are not very good at determining the herbal proportions, the herbalist can do it for you. Just tell him or her the number of people you intend to serve.

❖ Another way of cooking this dish is to first double-boil all the herbs for 2–3 hours, then discard herbs, except for boxthorn fruit and codonopsis root. Except for wine, shark's fin, sea cucumbers and abalone, combine all other ingredients and herbal liquid and double-boil for 4 hours. Lastly, add remaining ingredients and double-boil for 10–15 minutes more.

❖ Although double-boiling is the preferred way of cooking this dish, some people have opted for simmering as a more convenient way out.

Chinese angelica and donkey's glue

Serves 1–2

This is an excellent brew for addressing anaemia in general and promoting blood circulation. It can be off-putting for some, however, as it leaves a gluey, burnt after-taste.

Chinese angelica (*dang gui / dong kwai*)	4 slices
Donkey's glue (*e jiao / ah kau*)	½ block
Dried black dates (*hei zao / hak cho*)	15, stones removed
Water	750 ml (3 bowls)

✧ Combine all ingredients in a pot. Simmer for 2–3 hours or until liquid is halved. Drink warm.

Double-boiled chicken with Chinese angelica

Serves 1

This is a very potent tonic and extremely effective for various female disorders including painful periods, scanty periods and amenorrhoea. The potency of this brew lies in the fact that Chinese angelica has a high B12 vitamin content. Combined with old ginger which has excellent warming properties and the nutrients found in a chicken, this makes for a nourishing treat. In selecting chicken, it is best to use the breast or thigh as there is more meat.

Chicken	350 g, skinned, gristle removed, cut into average-size pieces, washed and dried
Old ginger	4-cm knob, crushed
Salt	1 pinch
Chinese angelica (*dang gui / dong kwai*)	15 g

✧ Combine chicken, ginger and salt.
✧ Place an inverted heatproof (flameproof) bowl into a bigger, upright heatproof bowl. Spread combined ingredients on top of inverted bowl. Put Chinese angelica along edge of upturned bowl. Double-boil for 4 hours.
✧ Every half hour, add a spoonful of water to chicken to prevent sticking or drying out. You should obtain 190–250 ml (¾–1 bowl) liquid at the end of cooking time. Drink this deliciously thick and rich brew before going to bed.

MOTHERHOOD
— Before and After Childbirth

Today's expectant mother is more aware that taking drugs during pregnancy can have adverse effects on the baby. When an expectant mother takes a drug, it enters her bloodstream and, in most cases, passes through the placenta to her unborn child. Since whatever an expectant mother consumes affects the formation of the foetus inside her, substances such as tobacco and alcohol and even minor tranquilisers should be avoided.

Exotic brews or tonics are not usually prescribed for pregnant women. To ensure an uneventful and trouble-free pregnancy, a nourishing, balanced and healthy diet is imperative. Vegetables that are cooling are to be avoided, as should sprouting potatoes because they are considered toxic to the system. The mother-to-be also has to abstain from 'sharp' fruits such as unripe mango and pineapple and keep away from cold food or drinks. It is said that lots of clear soups and brews can ensure baby's skin will be clear, smooth and problem-free.

Traditionally, a new mother was expected to abide by a very strict, restrictive diet and also some social taboos after birthing. In the twenty-first century, many women do not observe the confinement period as strictly as their predecessors did, if they do at all. During the confinement period, which can range from a month to 44 days, the new mother is advised to stay indoors, keep herself well wrapped up and be wary of coldness and winds or any atmospheric condition that is damp or wet. As a woman after childbirth is considered to be at her most susceptible and is sensitive to dampness or coldness, she has to follow a set of preventive guidelines that regulate not only her diet, but also her personal habits.

Firstly, she is put on a special, controlled diet to help her recover from the ordeal of giving birth. Hot broths and brews that strengthen her body, give warmth and get rid of wind and chills feature prominently in her diet. For obvious reasons, the main ingredients used in preparing foods for the mother in confinement are *yang* in energy and have stimulating and heating properties. Old ginger, sesame seed oil, garlic, onions, sweet vinegar, black peppercorns, red and black dates and rice wine are some such ingredients. Some traditionalists believe that rice wine should be used in moderation and only during the first 10 to 12 days after delivery and that an excess over a long period will burn up the liver. Most people, however, use rice wine for the entire confinement period.

Although the confinement diet is both boring and restrictive, it is a commonsense health programme. A lot of meats (chicken, pork and liver), eggs and fish — all *yang* foods — supply the new mother who has suffered a calcium loss through childbirth with a fresh store of it. Sweet vinegar dilates the blood vessels and improves circulation. It also helps the uterus to return to normal, expelling any blood clots left behind and also stimulating the liver and the production of bile, which improves digestion. A new mother who has a poor appetite will find difficulty in regaining her strength, energy and stamina.

Ginger, a stimulant, removes gases from the stomach and the intestinal tract. It is an invaluable source of nerve regeneration and offsets any potential chill following the excessive sweating that accompanies labour. The tonic qualities of ginger are so trusted that in the past, it was not uncommon for a woman in confinement to use up to 20 kilograms of old ginger in a 30-day period. This works out to more than 500 grams a day, which still pales in comparison to some women who use up to 500 grams in preparing just one dish.

For the woman in confinement, iced or cold drinks may cause severe shock to the system and should be dutifully avoided. This is why boiled, warm brews made from black and red dates, beans, livers and other meats are recommended as they help to heat up the womb. Three tonic herbs, in particular, are prescribed as musts for the new mother and they are astragalus root (*huang qi / puk kei*) to alleviate fatigue and improve blood circulation, Chinese angelica (*dang gui / dong kwai*) to alleviate pain and prevent haemorrhage and Chinese yam (*shan yao / wai san*) for its healing and revitalising qualities.

Pregnant women should be mindful of including dairy products, meat and eggs, vegetables, fruits, bread and cereals in their diet. Those who believe in tonics during the pregnancy period are wont to take prescriptions from herbalists but these are not without risks as western doctors often point out.

On the homefront, anxious mothers-in-law often prepare nutritious concoctions such as pig's stomach, fried kidneys and liver soups to build up the health of the expectant mother so that the baby will be both robust and healthy. It is also common practice for mothers, who want beautiful babies with smooth skins and complexions, to drink plenty of homemade soybean milk and sweet brews of barley, gingko nuts and soybean sticks.

* Unless otherwise stated, dishes in this section can be served for the entire confinement period.
* Unless otherwise stated, all dishes in this section are suitable for expectant mothers too. They are not musts, however, as general family fare contains enough tissue-building protein, vitamins and minerals for the average expectant mother.
* Expectant mothers who are inclined towards dishes in this section (only the ones they are recommended to consume) have to make the following changes:
  * exclude sesame seed oil and use other cooking oils as the former is too heating
  * reduce the amount of ginger used to only a few slices
  * omit wine when a recipe calls for it
  * reduce the amount of peppercorns to about one to two teaspoons when recipe calls for more
* New mothers are advised to confine their diet solely to the dishes in this section and as far as possible refrain from general family fare until the confinement period is over.
* All dishes, including tonics and teas, should be consumed fresh and on the same day they are cooked, never overnight.
* Some recipes in this section are for one, while others are for four to six servings. The former are solely for the expectant or new mother, and the latter for the whole family. During confinement, new mothers are normally given one dish per meal so portions are larger than normal.
* Teas and some tonics are prepared in large amounts because they are imbibed through the day in place of water. Store in a thermos flask to keep warm.

Recipes

Main Meals

Soups and noodles:
1. Chicken and boxthorn fruit soup p.133
2. Chinese angelica and chicken soup+ p.133
3. Liver soup p.134
4. Chicken and black fungus soup p.134
5. Double-boiled pig's brain with ginger juice and onions+ p.136
6. Lean pork, Chinese yam and cordyceps soup p.136
7. Fine vermicelli with kidneys p.138

Dishes:
1. Trotter in black vinegar p.139
2. Stir-fried liver with ginger p.140
3. Ginger fried chicken p.140
4. Pig's kidney with ginger and rice wine+ p.141
5. Fried pomfret with sliced ginger p.141
6. Drunken chicken+ p.142
7. Stir-fried pig's kidneys in sesame seed oil p.142
8. Ginger fried rice with egg p.144
9. Fried lean pork with ginger p.144
10. Stir-fried turmeric chicken+ p.145
11. Fried threadfin with ginger strips p.145
12. Omelette in rice wine p.146
13. Omelette with ginger p.146
14. Stir-fried French beans in sesame seed oil p.148
15. Steamed pomfret p.148
16. Fried chicken in turmeric juice+ p.149
17. Steamed chicken with ginger p.149
18. Crab with ginger and wine+ p.150
19. *Yim gok gai* (Salt-baked chicken)+ p.152
20. Pig's tripe with peppercorns p.154

Tonic brews and teas
1. Fried rice tea+ p.155
2. *Sung fah thong*+ p.155
3. Ginger juice+ p.156
4. Red and black date tea+ p.156
5. Dried longan and red date tea+ p.156

+ Not for expectant mothers.

Soups and noodles

Chicken and boxthorn fruit soup
Serves 4–6

When combined, chicken and boxthorn fruit, also known as Chinese wolfberries, are twin power boosters for depleted strength or low vitality. The soup is subtly sweet and very pleasant-tasting.

Chicken	1, about 1–1½ kg
Boxthorn fruit (*gou qi zi* / *gei chi*)	4 heaped Tbsp, washed and drained
Water	1½ l (6 bowls)
Salt	1 tsp
Pepper to taste	

✧ Clean chicken. Discard head, neck and legs. Skin, then cut into large pieces.

✧ Except for pepper, combine all other ingredients in a pot. Simmer for 3–4 hours. Add pepper to taste. Drink soup hot.

✧ Discard chicken if you do not like the flat taste of the meat. In herbal cooking, the belief is that all the goodness of the chicken would have already drained into the soup.

Chinese angelica and chicken soup
Serves 4–6
(Not suitable for expectant mothers)

Considered the most indispensable of all women's herbs because it builds blood, nourishes the womb and relieves a host of women's ills, Chinese angelica is generously used during the confinement period. If you are not too fussy about having an oil- and fat-free brew, cook chicken with skin intact.

Chicken thighs	3–4, about 1½ kg; skinned, washed and drained
Chinese angelica (*dang gui* / *dong kwai*)	35 g
Water	2 l (8 bowls)
Salt	½ tsp
Pepper to taste	

✧ Combine all ingredients in a large saucepan. Simmer for 2–3 hours over low heat. Drink warm.

Liver soup

Serves 1

Liver is high in iron and therefore a good source of strength and energy, especially for women undergoing confinement. Nursing mothers, however, should not consume liver in any form as it is said to dry up milk.

Sesame seed oil	1 Tbsp
Ginger	4-cm knob, well shredded
Water	500 ml (2 bowls)
Pig's liver	200 g, thinly sliced
Salt	1/4 tsp
Spring onion (scallion)	1 stalk, finely chopped
Pepper to taste	

◇ Heat sesame seed oil in a wok. Fry ginger until brown.
◇ Bring water to the boil in a saucepan. Add liver, salt and fried ginger. Simmer for 2–3 minutes. Serve hot.
◇ To serve, garnish with spring onion. Add pepper to taste.

Chicken and black fungus soup

Serves 1

Also known as wood ear fungus, black fungus is generously used in confinement dishes as it is believed to be effective in preventing blood from clotting.

Free range chicken	1, about 450 g
Dried black fungus	
(*hei mu er* / *mok yi*)	200 g
Sesame seed oil	2–3 Tbsp
Ginger	4-cm knob, finely sliced
Water	1 l (4 bowls)
Light soy sauce	1 Tbsp
Rice wine	3–4 Tbsp or more if preferred

◇ Clean chicken. Discard head, neck and legs. Cut into average-size pieces. Set aside.
◇ To prepare fungus, cut off hard roots. Wash, then soak in water for 45–60 minutes until soft. Slice into smaller pieces.
◇ Heat sesame seed oil in a wok. Add ginger and stir-fry a while. Add chicken and stir-fry a few minutes more. Remove.
◇ Transfer chicken to a saucepan. Add water and simmer for 20 minutes or until soft. Add fungus and soy sauce. Bring to the boil and sustain for 5 minutes. Add wine and remove immediately from heat. Serve hot.

Tip
❖ Traditionally, too much salt is considered unhealthy for the new mother. Soy sauce should be used instead.

Double-boiled pig's brain with ginger juice and onions

Serves 1
(Not suitable for expectant mothers).

Some new mothers suffer from rheumatism. When they shower or bathe, or wash their hair too frequently without regard to the weather conditions or time of day, they may later suffer from severe pains in the head. These painful headaches may be alleviated with this time-tested remedy which is still utilised by many. For all its rich goodness, this soup should not be consumed more than once a week.

Pig's brain	1, thoroughly cleaned (refer to p.90)	
Ginger juice	2–3 Tbsp, extracted from 2 4-cm knobs	
Onions	10, large; peeled, washed and left whole	
Water	500 ml (2 bowls)	
Salt	1/2 tsp	

◇ Except for salt, combine all other ingredients in a double-boiler or heatproof (flameproof) bowl. Double-boil for 4 hours. Add salt. Remove from heat.

◇ You should get about 250 ml (1 bowl) of liquid at the end of the cooking time. If preferred, remove the softened onions before serving. The key is to drink the soup and eat the pig's brains. Garnish with raw onion shreds if desired.

Lean pork, Chinese yam and cordyceps soup

Serves 4–6

Chinese yam relieves inflammation of the uterus, while cordyceps combat body aches and pains.

Lean pork	600 g, cut into large chunks
Chinese yam (*shan yao / wai san*)	30 g
Boxthorn fruit (*gou qi zi / gei chi*)	3 Tbsp
Cordyceps (*dong chong xia cao / tung chong cho*)	30 g
Water	2 l (8 bowls)
Salt	1/2 tsp or more to taste

◇ Combine all ingredients in a pot. Simmer for 3–4 hours. Serve hot.

Fine rice vermicelli with kidneys

Serves 4–6

When preparing this dish, it is of utmost importance that boiling soup is immediately poured over the vermicelli after it is scalded. The vermicelli turns into stodgy, starchy, inedible lumps if left for too long after being drained.

Pig's kidneys	1 pair, thoroughly cleaned
Rice wine	2 tsp
Sesame seed oil	3 Tbsp
Ginger	4-cm knob, finely shredded
Garlic	4 cloves, finely chopped
Boiling water	1^1/$_2$ l (6 bowls)
Salt	^{1}/$_2$ tsp
Light soy sauce	1 Tbsp
Fine rice vermicelli (*mian xian* / *meen seen*)	6 bundles
Spring onion (scallion)	1 stalk, finely chopped
Pepper to taste	

✧ Combine kidneys and wine in a bowl. Leave for 10–15 minutes.

✧ Heat sesame seed oil in wok. Fry ginger and garlic until light brown. Pour in boiling water. Add salt and soy sauce. Bring to the boil. Add kidneys, then turn off heat so as not to overcook kidneys.

✧ Scald rice vermicelli in sufficient boiling water for 30 seconds. Drain off excess water. Divide into 4–6 portions. Pour soup and kidney slices over rice vermicelli. Garnish with spring onion and add pepper to taste.

Tips

❖ Cleaning pig's kidneys can be quite a chore. To make it a little easier, have your butcher halve it horizontally for you and then cut out the central white membranes and urinary tubes.

❖ If cleaning them yourself, fill the hollow in the centre of each kidney with water from a running tap before cutting it into halves. Discard the membranes and urinary tubes and make criss-cross slits on kidney halves. This tenderises the kidneys and allows them to cook faster. Cut kidneys into 2-cm pieces, then soak them in cold water for up to 5 hours or even overnight in the refrigerator (keep covered) before cooking. Some people, however, maintain that soaking the kidneys overnight takes away the freshness and nutrients.

Trotter in black vinegar
Serves 4–6

This is standard fare for the confinement period, with black vinegar believed to encourage digestion, ginger to heat up a now 'cold' womb and trotter to promote strength. Palm sugar is used instead of refined, white sugar because the latter is believed to cause more wind than is healthy for a new mother. Palm sugar causes little to no wind.

Pig's trotter (foreleg)	1, about 1½ kg
Sesame seed oil	3 Tbsp
Old ginger	500–600 g, peeled, washed, pounded to break and cut into chunks
Garlic	3 cloves, crushed
Water	1¼ l (5 bowls)
Black vinegar	250 ml (1 bowl)
Palm sugar (*gula melaka*)	1 whole piece, soaked in hot water to soften and sieved
Salt to taste	

Tips

❖ Black vinegar in the dish acts to shorten the time it takes to soften the trotter.

❖ If you like your ginger with less bite, simmer the peeled ginger in hot water for 3 minutes, drain well, then fry in a dry wok. Remove when ginger has dried out. Heat a little oil in a wok. Add ginger, vinegar, salt and sugar. Simmer for 30 minutes before adding trotter pieces, which have to be fried in a little oil for 10–15 minutes first. Simmer for 20–30 minutes more or until meat is tender.

✧ Wash pig's trotter. Cut into average-size pieces. You can blanch trotter for about 20 minutes in boiling water and drain before cooking. This not only cuts cooking time, but also removes any leftover slime.

✧ Heat sesame seed oil in a wok. Fry ginger and garlic for 5 minutes. Add trotter pieces. Stir for 10 minutes. Transfer to a clay pot.

✧ Add sufficient water to cover trotter pieces. Bring to the boil. Simmer over low heat for 30 minutes. Add vinegar, sugar and salt. Simmer for 15–45 minutes more, depending on how soft you like the meat to become.

✧ Stir every few minutes so that meat does not stick to bottom of pot. Add liquid if necessary. Serve hot.

✧ For some, this dish is tastier if left overnight. To reheat, take out trotter pieces, bring liquid to the boil, then return trotter pieces. This prevents the meat from becoming overcooked and mushy.

Stir-fried liver with ginger

Serves 1

Since stir-frying is a quick process and permits only minimal alteration of the flavour and texture of the food, ingredients in any stir-fried dish should be as fresh as possible. This is especially so with liver. When well fried, liver should be brown outside and light coloured but very juicy inside. Liver that is overcooked has a hard and rubbery texture.

Pig's liver	200 g, thinly sliced
Light soy sauce	1 tsp
Crushed peppercorns	1/2 tsp
Salt	1/4 tsp
Sesame seed oil	2 Tbsp
Ginger	2 4-cm knobs, finely shredded
Shallot (optional)	1, small; sliced

✧ Season liver with soy sauce, peppercorns and salt. Set aside for a few minutes.

✧ Heat sesame seed oil in a wok. Add ginger and shallot if used. Fry for 2 minutes. Turn heat up and add liver. Stir-fry for 5 minutes. Dish out and serve immediately.

✧ For extra dash, add 2 Tbsp wine and 1 Tbsp water to remaining liver juice and oil (after transferring liver to a serving dish), stir for 2 minutes, then pour sauce over fried liver.

Ginger fried chicken

Serves 1

Although free range chickens are usually recommended in herbal cooking, this recipe is an exception. If a free range chicken is used to prepare this simple yet tasty dish, the resulting meat would be very tough.

Chicken	1, about 450 g; deboned and sliced
Dark soy sauce	1 Tbsp
Light soy sauce	1 Tbsp
Salt	1/2 tsp or more to taste
Garlic	1 clove, crushed
Sesame seed oil	3 Tbsp
Ginger	2 4-cm knobs, finely shredded
Stock or water	2 Tbsp
Pepper to taste	

✧ Season chicken with soy sauces, salt, garlic and 1 Tbsp sesame seed oil. Set aside for 30 minutes.

✧ Heat remaining sesame seed oil in a wok. Fry ginger until fragrant. Add chicken. Fry until golden brown. Reduce heat and cook until chicken is tender. Add stock or water. Increase heat, stir well and remove to serve. Add pepper to taste.

Pig's kidney with ginger and rice wine

Serves 1
(Not suitable for expectant mothers)

This dish is served immediately to a new mother after she has recovered sufficiently from the ordeal of labour to be able to consume her first meal, to strengthen her kidneys. If she is agreeable, she can be served the dish once or twice a week until the end of the confinement period. Many aged 50 years and older also find this dish a great tonic. For them, the dish acts to renew strength and energy.

Sesame seed oil	3 Tbsp
Ginger	3 4-cm knobs, finely shredded
Pig's kidneys	1 pair, thoroughly cleaned (refer to p.138)
Rice wine	250 ml (1 bowl)

✧ Heat sesame seed oil in a wok over high heat. When oil is hot, fry ginger until light brown. Maintain high temperature and add kidneys. Stir quickly a few times. Add rice wine. Bring to the boil. Serve hot.

✧ Be careful not to overcook kidneys or they turn hard and chewy.

Fried pomfret with sliced ginger

Serves 1

Pomfret	1, medium-size
Light soy sauce	1 Tbsp
Dark soy sauce	1/4 Tbsp
Salt	1/2 tsp
Pepper	1/4 tsp
Sesame seed oil	2 Tbsp
Old ginger	4-cm knob, finely shredded
Cooking oil for shallow-frying	

✧ Clean, wash and drain fish. Make 3 diagonal slits on either side of body.

✧ Season fish with soy sauces, salt and pepper. Set aside for 30 minutes.

✧ Heat sufficient oil in a wok for shallow-frying. Fry fish over moderate heat until golden brown and cooked through. Turn over and repeat. Remove and drain fish. Remove oil from wok.

✧ Heat sesame seed oil in wok. Add ginger. Fry until light brown. Use as garnish on top of fish. Serve hot.

Drunken chicken

Serves 1

(Not suitable for expectant mothers)

As far as possible, use free range chickens instead of battery hens. Do the same for the majority of dishes using chicken to be eaten by a new mother undergoing confinement. Vary the amount of rice wine according to your preference. If you like ginger, you can use up to 600 grams of it here.

Free range chicken	1, about 450 g
Sesame seed oil	3 Tbsp
Old ginger	4 4-cm knobs, finely shredded
Rice wine	200–250 ml ($^3/_4$–1 bowl)
Sugar (optional)	1 pinch
Water	250 ml (1 bowl)
Salt to taste	

✧ Clean chicken. Discard head, neck and legs. Cut into large pieces.

✧ Heat sesame seed oil in a wok or saucepan. Fry ginger until fragrant and light brown. Add chicken pieces. Stir for 3–5 minutes.

✧ Add rice wine and sugar if used. Bring to the boil. Add water, then salt to taste. Bring to another boil. Simmer until chicken is tender.

Tip

❖ Free range chickens tend to have tough meat which is why some people only drink the soup.

Stir-fried pig's kidneys in sesame seed oil

Serves 1

(For early confinement only)

New mothers who, for one reason or another, do not want too much rice wine in their food will find this recipe a more sober alternative to the previous one. The dish is essential after childbirth.

Sesame seed oil	3 Tbsp
Ginger	3 4-cm knobs, finely shredded
Pig's kidneys	1 pair, thoroughly cleaned (refer to p.138)
Water or stock	3 Tbsp
Brandy or whisky (optional)	1 dash

✧ Heat sesame seed oil in a wok over high heat. When oil is hot, fry ginger until light brown. Maintain high temperature and add kidneys. Stir briskly for 3 minutes. Add water or stock. Bring to the boil. Dish out.

✧ Eat dish hot with a dash of brandy or whisky for extra zest and added warmth to the system.

Ginger fried rice with egg
Serves 4–6

More ginger can be used if the new mother likes the taste. When frying with sesame seed oil, as is the case in this recipe, add one to two tablespoons more of it than when using ordinary cooking oil.

Sesame seed oil	6 Tbsp
Ginger	3 4-cm knobs, finely chopped
Garlic	2 cloves, finely chopped
Shallot	1, medium-size; finely chopped
Cooked rice	800 g
Eggs	3, well beaten, then seasoned with $^1/_2$ tsp salt and pepper to taste
Spring onions (scallions)	3 stalks, coarsely chopped
Light soy sauce	1 Tbsp

✧ Heat sesame seed oil in a wok. Add ginger. Fry for 1 minute. Add garlic and shallot. Fry for 1 minute more. Add rice and mix thoroughly. When rice is heated through, push to side of wok.

✧ Increase heat slightly, pour eggs onto centre of wok. Scramble until nearly set, then mix with rice. Season to taste. Before removing to serve, add spring onions and soy sauce.

Fried lean pork with ginger
Serves 1

Although it is beef that is usually stir-fried with ginger slices, lean pork is used here instead.

Lean pork	200 g, thinly sliced
Light soy sauce	1 Tbsp
Crushed peppercorns	$^1/_2$ tsp
Salt	$^1/_4$ tsp
Sesame seed oil	2 Tbsp
Ginger	2 4-cm knobs, finely shredded
Shallot	1, small; sliced

✧ Season pork with soy sauce, peppercorns and salt. Set aside for 15–20 minutes.

✧ Heat oil in a wok. Fry ginger and shallot until brown. Increase heat and add pork. Stir-fry until meat is cooked through. Serve hot.

Tip
❖ You can add a little rice wine for extra zest before dishing out the fried pork.

Stir-fried turmeric chicken

Serves 4–6
(Not for expectant mothers)

Like ginger, turmeric has both healing and warming properties.

Free range chicken	1, about 450 g
Shallots	4–5, peeled
Lemon grass	4–5 stalks, cut into 3-cm lengths
Turmeric	2 4-cm knobs, peeled and sliced
Peppercorns	1 Tbsp
Sesame seed oil	2–3 Tbsp
Light soy sauce	1 Tbsp
Salt to taste	

✧ Clean chicken. Discard head, neck and legs. Cut into average-size pieces.

✧ Grind (process) shallots, lemon grass, turmeric and peppercorns into a paste. Marinate chicken pieces in paste for at least 1 hour.

✧ Heat sesame seed oil in a wok. Fry marinated chicken until cooked. Add soy sauce and salt to taste. If dish dries up too quickly, add 1 Tbsp water. Serve hot.

Fried threadfin with ginger strips

Serves 1

Threadfins are expensive and usually sold in steaks.

Threadfin	1, medium-size, about 400 g; washed and drained
Light soy sauce	1 Tbsp
Dark soy sauce	1/4 Tbsp
Salt and pepper to taste	
Sesame seed oil	2 Tbsp
Old ginger	2-cm knob, finely shredded
Cooking oil for shallow-frying fish	

✧ Season fish with soy sauces and salt and pepper to taste. Set aside for 30 minutes.

✧ Heat sufficient oil in a wok for shallow-frying. Fry fish over moderate heat until golden brown and cooked through. Remove and drain fish. Remove oil from wok.

✧ Heat sesame seed oil in wok. Add ginger. Fry until fragrant and light brown. Use as garnish on top of fish. Serve immediately.

Omelette in rice wine

Serves 1

Sesame seed oil	3–4 Tbsp
Old ginger	3 4-cm knobs, finely shredded
Eggs	2, well beaten
Rice wine	250 ml (1 bowl)

✧ Heat sesame seed oil in a wok. Add ginger and fry until light brown. Spread out ginger evenly. Add eggs. Scramble well until nearly set. Add wine. Bring to the boil. Reduce heat and simmer for a few minutes more. Serve hot.

Tip

❖ Rice wine has to be heated until boiling to prevent indigestion or stomachaches. This is especially important considering the delicate constitution of a new mother.

Omelette with ginger

Serves 1

Since eggs are believed to delay the healing of stitched wounds, some new mothers who have had surgery in the course of delivery avoid eating eggs. This recipe calls for an equal proportion of ginger to egg. Reduce amount of ginger to suit personal taste.

Sesame seed oil	3 Tbsp
Ginger	3 4-cm knobs, finely shredded
Garlic	1 clove, finely chopped
Shallot	1, medium-size; finely chopped
Eggs	2, well beaten
Light soy sauce	$1/2$ tsp

✧ Heat sesame seed oil in a pan. Add ginger. Fry for 1 minute. Add garlic and shallot. Fry for 1 minute more. Spread out browning ingredients evenly.
✧ Pour beaten eggs over ingredients. Toss until cooked. Dish out.
✧ Serve hot with soy sauce.

Stir-fried French beans in sesame seed oil

Serves 1

Sesame seed oil	3 Tbsp
Garlic	2 cloves, crushed and skins removed
French beans	250 g, washed, drained and cut into 2-cm lengths
Chicken stock	2 Tbsp
Salt and pepper to taste	

✧ Heat sesame seed oil in a wok. Add garlic. Fry until fragrant. Add French beans and stir. Pour stock over beans. Add salt and pepper to taste. Stir for 2 minutes more. Dish out and serve immediately.

Steamed pomfret

Serves 1

Although the usual time for steaming fish is about 10 to 15 minutes, it varies according to size, freshness and amount of heat applied.

White pomfret	1, medium-size
Old ginger	3-cm knob, finely chopped
Salt	$1/2$ tsp or more to taste
Light soy sauce	1 Tbsp
Sesame seed oil	2 Tbsp
Dried Chinese mushrooms	2, soaked, stems removed and thinly sliced
Spring onion (scallion)	1 stalk, cut into 2-cm lengths

✧ Clean, wash and drain fish. Make 2 slits on either side of body. Rub inside and out with ginger and salt. Set aside for 30 minutes.

✧ Season fish with soy sauce and sesame seed oil. Set aside for 30 minutes.

✧ Place fish on a heatproof (flameproof) dish. Pour remaining soy sauce mixture over fish. Decorate with mushroom slices.

✧ In a wok or large pot, bring sufficient water for steaming to an intense boil. Position steaming rack, then place dish with fish on top. Cover and steam for 10–15 minutes. Garnish with spring onions. Serve immediately.

Fried chicken in turmeric juice

Serves 4–6

(Not for expectant mothers)

This dish is *yang* in energy. Ideally, a free range chicken should be used and do not add too much turmeric juice or the meat will taste slightly bitter.

Chicken	1, about 1 kg
Peppercorns	10, crushed
Whole onions	3, large; peeled
Garlic	1 clove, peeled
Salt	1 tsp
Turmeric juice	extracted from 4 4-cm knobs
Sesame seed oil	5 Tbsp
Rice wine or water	2–3 Tbsp

- ✧ Clean chicken. Discard head, neck and legs. Cut into average-size pieces.
- ✧ Grind (process) peppercorns, onions, garlic and salt together. Mix in turmeric juice.
- ✧ Marinate chicken pieces in ground mixture for 2–3 hours.
- ✧ Heat sesame seed oil in a wok. Fry marinated chicken, turning frequently until meat is tender. If dish dries up too quickly, add rice wine or water. Keep heat low to prevent burning. Serve hot.

Steamed chicken with ginger

Serves 1

Chicken	1, about 450 g
Sesame seed oil	3 Tbsp
Onion	1, large; sliced
Garlic	1 clove, peeled and sliced
Old ginger	200 g, peeled and finely chopped or blended (processed)
Salt	$1/2$ tsp or more to taste
Pepper	$1/2$ tsp
Rice wine	2 Tbsp

- ✧ Clean chicken. Discard head, neck and legs. Skin and remove excess fat. Cut into average-size pieces.
- ✧ Heat sesame seed oil in a wok. Brown onion and garlic. Remove from wok and set aside
- ✧ In a bowl, combine ginger, salt, pepper and rice wine. Add fried onion and garlic. Mix well.
- ✧ Put chicken pieces into a heatproof (flameproof) dish. Spread ginger mixture on and around chicken pieces. Steam for 30–45 minutes. Chicken will cook in its own juices. Serve hot.

Crab with ginger and wine

Serves 1

(Not for expectant mothers)

Women undergoing confinement usually abstain from flower crabs, but crabs with more flesh are allowed. New mothers who have had surgery performed on them during delivery, however, should abstain from all kinds of crabs because seafood in general is believed to deter the healing of wounds.

Crabs	2, large, about 1 kg
Rice wine	2 Tbsp
Stock or water	1 Tbsp
Cornflour (cornstarch)	2 Tbsp; replaceable with 1 small, well beaten egg
Sesame seed oil	4 Tbsp
Old ginger	2 4-cm knobs, finely sliced
Spring onions (scallions)	2 stalks, finely chopped
Dark soy sauce	1 Tbsp
Sugar	1 tsp
Salt	1 tsp

✧ Clean and wash crabs. Remove top shells, then cut into halves. Crack shells covering claws. Break off legs.

✧ Combine 1 Tbsp rice wine and stock or water, then mix in cornflour. Season crab pieces with combined ingredients.

✧ Heat sesame seed oil in a wok. Add crab pieces. Fry for about 2 minutes. Add ginger, spring onions, soy sauce, sugar, salt and remaining rice wine. Cook for 5 minutes, stirring continuously. If dish dries up too quickly, add a little more stock or water. Dish out and serve hot.

Yim gok gai (Salt-baked chicken)

Serves 4–6

(Not for expectant mothers)

Salt-baked chicken or *yim gok gai* in Cantonese is a very nutritious and also heating dish.
It was traditionally prepared for new mothers undergoing confinement but has since also been treated as
gourmet fare by some who appreciate its special taste. A free range chicken is recommended if being
cooked for a new mother.

Free range chicken	1, about 1 kg
Sesame seed oil	1 Tbsp; replaceable with 1 Tbsp rice wine
Salt	1/2 tsp
Ginger	2 4-cm knobs, finely sliced
Shallots	2–3, peeled and crushed
Coarse salt	3 kg
Eggs	4, hard-boiled and shelled

- ✧ Wash and drain chicken well. On inside of chicken, first brush on sesame seed oil or rice wine, rub 1/2 tsp salt, then spread ginger and shallots all over.
- ✧ Fry coarse salt in an old wok for 30 minutes or until very hot and jumping.
- ✧ Put boiled eggs inside chicken. Wrap chicken with 2 thick layers of greaseproof paper. Bury parcel completely in salt, making sure that an even layer covers the top.
- ✧ Place entire setup over a charcoal burner or into the oven. Bake for 30–45 minutes.
- ✧ When done, remove eggs from chicken. Serve eggs and chicken whole.

Tip

- ❖ The chicken should be baked in an old, disused wok as the salt will irreparably damage the wok by eventually causing extensive rust. Alternatively, fry the salt in your usual wok and transfer to a clay pot to bake.
- ❖ If preferred, separately wrap eggs in greaseproof paper and bury in salt alongside the chicken. This way, you can also cook more eggs.

Pig's tripe with peppercorns

Serves 4–6

Pig's tripe is considered a delicacy. When prepared properly, it is relished by young and old. There are two versions of this dish, the simpler, soup version (below) and the family version that has more complementing ingredients such as gingko nuts, bean curd sticks, mushrooms and water chestnuts. The simpler version is, nevertheless, a hearty, heating and invigorating soup. New mothers are served this version to revive and stimulate their drained bodies. The added ingredients in the family version make for a wholesome and rich meal for all members of the household, including the expectant mother.

Pig's tripe	1, thoroughly cleaned (refer to p.109)
Peppercorns	30, washed and crushed
Chicken carcasses	2, washed and drained
Pork bones (optional)	200 g
Water	2 l (8 bowls)
Salt to taste	

✧ Combine all ingredients in a large pot. Cover and simmer for 1–1¹⁄₂ hours. Remove tripe and drain. Slice into small pieces. Serve alongside soup.

✧ If you find the tripe slices somewhat tasteless, stir-fry them in some oil with onions and garlic, then serve alongside soup.

Tip

❖ There are 3 ways of using peppercorns in this dish:

1. Put them into tripe. Sew up tripe. This makes for a hot-tasting stomach.
2. Put into a small muslin bag. Sew or tie up, then add to the pot. This will prevent crushed pieces of peppercorns from floating about in the soup.
3. Just add peppercorns to the liquid. They will float freely and add zest to the soup.

Fried rice tea

Serves 1
(Not for expectant mothers)

Some people know this drink as the poor man's version of longan and red date tea. This aromatic brew, however, is not only nutritious and very warming to the body, but also easy to prepare, with no stones to remove. It also adds variety to an otherwise limited range of teas.

Rice (A1 grade)	½–1 kg, depending on personal requirements

- ✧ Sieve rice to remove grit.
- ✧ Toast rice grains in a dry wok until dark brown. Keep heat very low to prevent burning.
- ✧ Store fried rice grains in airtight containers. When required, put a handful or so of rice into a porcelain bowl or mug, then pour boiling hot water over the top. Cover to leach for a while. Drink warm 2–3 times a day in place of water.

Sung fah thong

Serves 1
(To be drunk only once during early confinement)

This traditional confinement brew is usually prescribed to a new mother two to three days after delivery. Slightly bitter in taste and blackish in colour, the powerful concoction is believed to cleanse the womb of any remaining blood clots and strengthen the lining of the womb. The formula of this brew is considered a trade secret among herbalists.

Sung fah thong	1 prescription
Water	1 l (4 bowls)

- ✧ Combine prescription and water in a clay pot. Simmer over low charcoal heat for 4 hours or until liquid is reduced to 250 ml (1 bowl). Drink warm.

Ginger juice

Serves 1

(Not for expectant mothers)

Not all new mothers are able to stomach this beverage which is considered the best remedy for wind, as well as for bringing on a good appetite. Drink once or twice during the confinement period. If there is a lot of wind, however, consume once every two to three days.

Ginger	120 g, peeled and cut into small slices	✧ Use a juice extractor to obtain ginger juice. Warm juice over low heat.
		✧ Drink warm, in between sips of black and red date tea or dried longan and red date tea.

Red and black date tea

Serves 1

(Not for expectant mothers)

Women undergoing confinement are usually advised not to drink plain water as this leads to bloating from water retention. This may explain the various brews, soups and teas specially designed for new mothers.

Dried red dates (*hong zao / hung cho*)	30, stones removed	✧ Combine all ingredients in a saucepan. Simmer over low heat for 1–2 hours. Drink warm and if preferred, throughout the day in place of water.
Dried black dates (*hei zao / hak cho*)	30, stones removed	✧ If you do not like eating cooked dates, drain and squeeze them for juice to return to brew before discarding pulp.
Water	2 l (8 bowls)	
Rock sugar	100 g	

Dried longan and red date tea

Serves 1

(Not for expectant mothers)

For people who dislike the taste of black dates, substitute with dried longan which has warming properties and is excellent for the heart, kidneys and spleen. This tea is equally good for new mothers and for anyone suffering from general weakness and anaemia. This drink is recommended for the entire confinement period.

Dried red dates (*hong zao / hung cho*)	50, stones removed	✧ Combine all ingredients in a saucepan. Simmer over low heat for 1–2 hours. Drink warm.
Water	2 l (8 bowls)	
Rock sugar	100 g	
Dried longan flesh	100 g, washed and drained	

FULL MOON FARE

The day a newborn turns one month old is an auspicious, festive occasion in a traditional Chinese household. The Chinese term for the occasion — *man yue / moon yuet* — literally translates into "full moon". Full moon fare, then, refers to the dishes that are customarily prepared for the occasion and served at home to a modest gathering of close relatives and friends. Special full moon dishes are also prepared and distributed to those who, for one reason or another, cannot attend the gathering.

Among the dishes served during the gathering would be the standard few that a new mother is given during her confinement period, eg chicken in rice wine and ginger, trotter in black vinegar and red date tea. Since the confinement diet excludes a variety of tabooed ingredients, food suited to a new mother can be bland at best and so when cooked for baby's full moon, the same dishes are made more flavourful and enjoyable by the addition of other ingredients. Other dishes that make up full moon fare are typically geared towards the guests, who are not subjected to any food-related taboos and, unlike the new mother, can eat without fear of food-induced ailments such as headaches or wind.

Red eggs and pickled ginger slices, especially, are synonymous with a baby's full moon. The Hokkien Chinese, in particular, favour a traditional sweet treat of sweetened green (mung) bean paste wrapped with a red, chewy skin for the occasion. Called *kuih angku* by the Peranakan or Straits Chinese, the red sweet, alongside similarly coloured eggs and dried dates, is supposed to represent all things prosperous, happy and joyous. In fact, for some, the *kuih* is made round if the newborn is a girl and bolster-shaped if a boy. The phallic symbol here is overtly evident.

Aside from these staples, other dishes are prepared and served according to the beliefs and customs of the baby's family. With time and cross-cultural influences, different households have come to include different dishes in the marking of a baby's full moon. The Peranakan people, for example, prepare the fragrant *nasi kunyit* (yellow glutinous rice) with a chicken curry.

Full moon dishes are served together as a varied luncheon. In this section, a sample menu ample for a party of 15 to 18 people has been provided. If you have guests who are unaccustomed to hot or spicy dishes, replace *nasi kunyit* with chicken-flavoured rice, or have both so that there is an alternative.

It is also customary for parents of a newborn to have four to five food items delivered to relatives and friends who are unable to attend the celebration of their baby's full moon. In this respect, red eggs, pickled ginger slices, roast pork and boiled chicken are full moon classics. For the Peranakan or Straits Chinese, including *nasi kunyit* and chicken curry in the delivered package is also an accepted practice.

Recipes

Sample Menu
1. *Chap chye* (Mixed vegetable special) p.161
2. Trotter with sea cucumbers and mushrooms p.162
3. Chicken, boxthorn fruit and Solomon's seal soup p.164
4. Dried longan and red date tea p.164
5. Fried noodle special p.165
6. Savoury pig's tripe p.165
7. Preserved young ginger p.166
8. Red eggs p.166
9. *Nasi kunyit* (Yellow glutinous rice) p.168
10. Chicken curry p.170

Other Recipes
1. *Bak cham gai* (Boiled chicken) p.171
2. Chicken-flavoured rice and soup p.172
3. Beans and peanuts with chicken in wine p.173

Chap chye (Mixed vegetable special)

This is a nutritious health platter that combines a number of vegetables and protein-rich ingredients that have been selected to symbolise harmony, prosperity, good luck and longevity. The choice of ingredients to include here, however, is really flexible. Non-vegetarians, for example, can add prawns (shrimps) and lean meat if desired. This dish was once only served during special occasions but has since become a favourite family dish.

Cabbage	30 g, cut into segments
Carrots	30 g, cut into 4-cm lengths and then thinly sliced
Cauliflower	30 g, cut into florets
Cooking oil	2–3 Tbsp
Dried lily buds (golden needles)	30 g, hard tips removed, individually knotted and soaked to soften
Dried bean curd sticks (*fu zhu / fu chok*)	3, broken into 4-cm lengths and soaked
Transparent vermicelli (*fen si / fun see*)	30 g, soaked to soften
Dried black fungus (*hei mu er /mok yi*)	20 g, soaked, hard roots removed and cut into bite-size pieces
Dried cloud ear fungus (*yun er / wun yi*)	20 g, soaked, hard roots removed and cut into bite-size pieces
Dried Chinese mushrooms	6, soaked, stems removed and thickly sliced
Red fermented bean curd (*nan ru /nam yue*)	2 pieces
Celery	3 sticks, cut into 3-cm lengths
Snow peas	30 g
Canned bamboo shoots	½ can, drained
*Seasoning mixture	1 recipe

◇ Parboil cabbage, carrots and cauliflower. Set aside.

◇ Heat oil in a wok. Add lily buds and parboiled ingredients. Stir-fry for 2–3 minutes.

◇ Add all remaining ingredients, then seasoning mixture last. Stir well. Simmer for 3–5 minutes or until ingredients are cooked. Serve hot.

---

*Seasoning mixture:

Sugar	1 tsp
Stock	250 ml (1 bowl)
Salt	½ tsp or more to taste
Light soy sauce	1 Tbsp
Dark soy sauce	1 Tbsp
Sesame seed oil	1 Tbsp
Oyster sauce	1 Tbsp

◇ Combine all ingredients in a bowl. Mix well.

Trotter with sea cucumbers and mushrooms

A richer and more savoury way of cooking trotter than that served to the
new mother (p.139), this dish will appeal to a wider range of palates.

Pig's trotter (foreleg)	1, about 1$^1/_2$ kg
Sesame seed oil	2 Tbsp
Garlic	4 cloves, crushed and diced
Ginger	4-cm knob, crushed and sliced
Water	1$^1/_2$ l (6 bowls)
Rice wine	2 Tbsp
Dark soy sauce	1 Tbsp
Light soy sauce	1 Tbsp
Salt	1 tsp
Dried sea cucumbers	6, soaked in water overnight, thoroughly cleaned and cut into smaller pieces if desired
Dried Chinese mushrooms	20–25, soaked, stems removed and halved or quartered
Red chillies	4, thinly sliced

✧ Wash trotter. Cut into average-size pieces. Blanch trotter pieces in boiling water for about 10 minutes. Rinse off all traces of grease. Drain well.

✧ Heat sesame seed oil in a wok. Fry garlic and ginger. Add trotter pieces. Fry for 10 minutes.

✧ Transfer to a clay pot. Add water, wine, soy sauces and salt. Simmer for 45 minutes or until meat is almost tender.

✧ Add sea cucumbers and mushrooms. Simmer 10–15 minutes more. Serve hot with chillies.

Tips

❖ Most herbal shops sell dried sea cucumbers that have already been cleaned and require only soaking and moderate cleaning before cooking. Sea cucumbers can expand up to 3 times their dried up size. Some supermarkets sell cleaned, fresh sea cucumbers and these can be used after rinsing.

❖ If preparing sea cucumbers from their dried but unprocessed state, soak them for up to a week before cooking, with 2–3 changes of water a day to get rid of the grit and embedded slime. You can also scrape the soaked sea cucumber clean with a knife or toast them over a charcoal flame to dislodge the dirt.

Chicken, boxthorn fruit and Solomon's seal soup

This recipe is for a clear, tasty and nutritious soup. If you dislike even the smallest hint of oiliness, skin the chicken.

Chicken	1, about 1¹/₂ kg
Solomon's seal (*yu zhu / yok chok*)	30 g
Boxthorn fruit (*gou qi zi / gei chi*)	4 Tbsp
Dried Chinese mushrooms	20, soaked, stems removed and cut into small pieces
Water	2 l (8 bowls)
Salt	¹/₂ tsp or more to taste
Peppercorns	1 tsp

✧ Clean chicken. Discard head, neck and legs. Trim off excess fat. Cut into average-size pieces.
✧ Combine all ingredients in saucepan. Simmer for 3–4 hours. Serve hot.

Dried longan and red date tea

This traditional brew is usually served to elders on auspicious occasions, especially during lunar new year. A cup of this tea, when offered, conveys wishes of good health and longevity. Red dates are preferred to black dates because the colour red represents joy, happiness and all things positive.

Dried longan flesh	250 g, soaked to soften and grit removed
Dried red dates (*hong zao / hung cho*)	50, stones removed
Water	2¹/₂ l (10 bowls)

✧ Combine all ingredients in a saucepan or, better still, a slow cooker. Simmer for 4–6 hours.
✧ At the end of the cooking time, remove ³/4 of dates. Squeeze for liquid to return to brew and discard pulp. Serve tea warm with a date or two and some longan.

Fried noodle special

Fried noodles are normally served for festive occasions such as a baby's full moon, which is a direct translation of the Chinese term for the day a baby turns one month old. This is because long lengths of the noodles signify long life.

Cooking oil	2 Tbsp
Garlic	4 cloves, crushed and diced
Streaky pork	300 g, cut into thin strips
Prawns (shrimps)	300 g, shelled
Stock	3 l (12 bowls)
Dark soy sauce	1 tsp
Light soy sauce	1 tsp
Salt to taste	
Fresh Hokkien noodles	500 g, scalded and drained
Bean sprouts	400 g, cleaned and blanched
Eggs	2, beaten, fried into an omelette and shredded
Crisp-fried shallots	4 Tbsp
Red chillies	5, finely sliced
Spring onions (scallions)	4 stalks, finely chopped
Pepper to taste	

✧ Heat oil in a wok. Add garlic and stir-fry. Add pork and prawns. Fry until cooked. Remove from wok. Set aside.

✧ Bring stock to the boil. Add soy sauces and salt to taste.

✧ Meanwhile, transfer noodles onto a large serving dish. Evenly distribute bean sprouts and fried pork and prawns over the top. Garnish with omelette shreds, shallot and chilli slices and spring onions. Pour stock over noodles. Add pepper to taste. Serve.

Savoury pig's tripe

Pig's tripe	1, thoroughly cleaned (refer to p.109)
Dried bean curd sticks (*fu zhu / fu chok*)	4–5, broken into 4-cm lengths and soaked
Gingko nuts (*bai guo / bak gor*)	30–40, shelled
Dried chestnuts	30–40, shelled and soaked
Salt	1 tsp or more to taste
Peppercorns	1 tsp
Water	2 l (8 bowls)
Abalone	1 can, thinly sliced

✧ Except for abalone, combine all other ingredients in a pot. Simmer over low heat for 1 hour.

✧ Add abalone. Simmer for 30 minutes more or until meats are soft. Serve hot.

Preserved young ginger

To make the finest preserved ginger, use only the youngest and freshest rhizome shoots because they contain very little fibre. The vinegar used should also be of good quality.

Young ginger	1 kg, peeled and sliced wafer thin
Salt	3 Tbsp
Vinegar	500 ml (2 bowls)
Sugar	150 g

- ✧ Rinse ginger slices clean and drain. Put into glass or porcelain container. Add salt and mix well. Cover and leave for 5 minutes. This reduces the ginger's hotness.
- ✧ Rinse ginger slices. Drain well. Leave to dry in the sun for 15 minutes.
- ✧ Put dried ginger slices into a saucepan. Add vinegar and sugar. Stir over low heat until sugar melts and is absorbed by ginger. Remove and leave to cool.
- ✧ Pack ginger slices into jars. Leave to soak for 2–3 days before serving.

Red eggs

This recipe is good for 15 to 18 eggs. Buy red food colouring powder from the herbal shop.

Water for boiling eggs	2 l
Fresh eggs	15–18
Red food colouring powder	3–4 Tbsp
Water	125 ml (1/2 bowl)
Vinegar	3 tsp
Salt	1 tsp

- ✧ Bring water to the boil in a large saucepan. Add salt. Place eggs in a small rattan basket. Lower basket into boiling water. Cover and keep boiling for 7–9 minutes. Remove eggs. Leave to cool.
- ✧ Put food colouring powder into a bowl. Add 125 ml water. Mix well until a fairly thick, smooth consistency is obtained. Add vinegar. Mix again. Dip boiled egg one by one into mixture. Roll it around to get an even colour on the shell. Put aside. Repeat for all the eggs.

Tip
- ✧ Cooking eggs in violently bubbling boiling water can cause them to crack by knocking either against each other or the side of the pot. The purpose of the small rattan basket is to prevent cracked eggs.

Nasi kunyit (Yellow glutinous rice)

Bright yellow in colour, this fragrant rice dish is delicious eaten with chicken curry.
The Peranakan or Straits Chinese usually distribute *nasi kunyit* and chicken curry to friends and relatives
together with red eggs to celebrate a baby's full moon.

Glutinous rice	600 g, washed and drained
Turmeric juice	1 Tbsp, extracted from 4-cm knob and sufficient water
Turmeric powder	2 tsp
Lemon juice (optional)	1 Tbsp
Salt	1/2 tsp
Water	250 ml (1 bowl)
Coconut	1/2, grated
Screwpine (*pandan*) leaves	4, knotted in pairs
Peppercorns (optional)	50, washed and drained

Tips

❖ If you are using a steamer, you may wish to place a cleaned banana leaf over the holes before placing the rice bowl on top for added fragrance.
❖ Whether to add lemon juice and/or peppercorns really depends on individual preference. Some people find that the lemon juice leaves a slightly bitter aftertaste, while others feel that the added fragrance imparted by the peppercorns is outweighed by the nuisance of biting into them when eating.
❖ Health conscious cooks can replace the freshly squeezed coconut milk in this recipe with the prepacked, low-fat variety.

◆ Combine rice, turmeric juice and powder, lemon juice if used and salt. Stir well for 5–10 minutes to mix. Cover and leave overnight or for at least 7–8 hours.
◆ Add 3 Tbsp water to grated coconut. Squeeze for thick coconut milk and set aside. Add remaining water to grated coconut. Squeeze for thin coconut milk. Set aside.
◆ If lemon juice is not used, put rice into a bowl, add thin coconut milk and stir well. If used, rinse and drain rice first. Mix in peppercorns if used. Top with screwpine leaves. Cover and steam for 25 minutes or longer if required. To steam, either a steamer or heatproof (flameproof) container can be used.
◆ When rice is nearly cooked, stir in thick coconut milk. Steam for 5–10 minutes more or until rice is cooked through. Serve with chicken curry (see following recipe).

Chicken curry

For the Peranakan or Straits Chinese, chicken curry and *nasi kunyit* traditionally went hand in hand. As this recipe is intended for guests and not tonic purposes, use regular chickens instead of free range ones for a juicier, tastier result.

Chicken	1, about 1$\frac{1}{2}$ kg
Garlic	10 cloves, chopped
Shallots	10, sliced
Dried chillies	10, seeded and soaked
Turmeric	4-cm knob
Cooking oil	4 Tbsp
Lemon grass	3 stalks, crushed after removing fibrous leaves
Curry leaves	1 sprig, washed
Curry powder	4 Tbsp, mixed with 4 Tbsp water to form a paste
Potatoes	4, peeled and halved
Thick coconut milk	125 ml ($\frac{1}{2}$ bowl), extracted from 1 grated coconut and sufficient water
Thin coconut milk	750 ml (3 bowls), extracted from same, used grated coconut and sufficient water
Salt	$\frac{1}{2}$ tsp or more to taste

◇ Clean chicken. Discard head, neck and legs. Cut into large pieces.
◇ Grind (process) garlic, shallots, chillies and turmeric to a rough paste. Set aside.
◇ Heat oil in a wok or saucepan. Add ground ingredients, lemon grass, curry leaves and paste. Reduce heat. Fry paste until fragrant and oil bubbles through. Add chicken. Fry for 10 minutes. Add thin coconut milk. Stir for 5 minutes. Add potatoes. Cover and simmer for 10 minutes.
◇ Add thick coconut milk. Bring to the boil and sustain for 5 minutes or until chicken is tender. Add salt. Serve hot.

Tips
❖ If a thinner gravy is preferred, add more water when squeezing for thin coconut milk to yield an extra 125–250 ml ($\frac{1}{2}$–1 bowl).
❖ Health conscious cooks can replace the freshly squeezed coconut milk in this recipe with the prepacked, low-fat variety.

Bak cham gai (Boiled chicken)

Traditional chicken rice, a popular meal in Singapore and Malaysia, consisted of pieces of
bak cham gai atop a serve of chicken-flavoured rice. Chicken rice is accompanied by a special chilli
sauce and soup made from the liquid used to boil the chicken.

Chicken	1, about 2 kg
Water	3 l (12 bowls)
Cucumber	1, large; cut into wedges

✧ Clean chicken. Leave whole after removing
   entrails.

✧ Bring water to the boil. Lower chicken into
   boiling water. Ensure that liquid covers chicken
   completely. Cover and let boil for 15 minutes.
   When cooked, remove chicken and leave to
   cool. Reserve liquid; it will be used in preparing
   an accompanying soup and chicken rice.

✧ Restaurant cooks and chicken rice sellers usually
   rinse the boiled chicken under a running tap to
   cool chicken faster so that its meat will not
   break up when chopped. For home
   consumption, this is unnecessary. In fact, rinsing
   will wash away some of its taste.

✧ Chop cooled chicken into small pieces. Arrange
   on a serving dish. Serve with cucumber wedges.

Chilli sauce for boiled chicken:

Kaffir limes	
(*limau purut*)	3, small
Red chillies	5, washed and seeded
Garlic	5 cloves, bruised and diced
Ginger	2 4-cm knobs, sliced
Sugar	1/2 tsp
Salt	1/2 tsp

✧ Halve limes. Squeeze for juice and set aside.
   Boil 3 lime halves in sufficient water for
   10 minutes until skin softens and splits. Remove
   and reserve skins. Discard liquid.

✧ Combine boiled lime skins, chillies, garlic and
   ginger. Pound with pestle and mortar or blend
   (process) until almost fine. Add sugar and salt
   to taste.

✧ For added chicken flavour, add 1 tsp hot chicken
   fat if desired. Add juice to chilli mixture. Mix
   well and it is ready to serve.

Chicken-flavoured rice and soup

Rice has been a staple food among the Chinese for thousands of years. Such was its importance that it was used in ancient China not only as food, but also as currency. It is also a symbol of fertility and was customarily pelted on newlyweds to wish them luck. The chicken stock called for in this recipe ideally should be the liquid reserved from boiling the chicken in the previous recipe.

Chicken fat	4–5 Tbsp
Garlic	10 cloves, finely diced
Young ginger	4-cm knob, crushed
Shallots	3, peeled and thinly sliced
Chicken stock	about 2½ l (10 bowls)
Rice	600 g, washed and drained
Salt	½ tsp

- ◇ Heat chicken fat in a wok. Fry garlic, ginger and shallots. Remove oil mixture and add to chicken stock.
- ◇ Bring stock to the boil. Sustain for 5 minutes. Strain stock to remove fried ingredients.
- ◇ Into a rice cooker or pot, add sufficient stock to rice and begin cooking.
- ◇ Meanwhile, heat remaining stock for soup. Add salt. When stock is hot, remove and garnish with bean sprouts or fried shallots. Add salt and pepper to taste.
- ◇ When done, serve rice and soup alongside boiled chicken and chilli sauce.

Beans and peanuts with chicken in wine

The origin of this dish is obscure and only certain dialect groups serve this during
a baby's full moon.

Chicken	1, about 1¹/₂ kg
Broad beans	30 g, soaked in water overnight, skins removed with a sharp knife, then rinsed and drained
Red adzuki beans	30 g, soaked in water for 2–3 hours and drained
Hyacinth beans	30 g, soaked in water for 2–3 hours and drained
Black-eyed beans	30 g, soaked in water for 2–3 hours and drained
Black beans	30 g, toasted in a dry nonstick pan until jumping, then swirled under a running tap and drained
Peanuts (groundnuts)	30 g, soaked in water for 2–3 hours, skins rubbed off and drained
Young ginger	4-cm knob, finely sliced
Water	375 ml (1¹/₂ bowls)
Cooking oil	2 Tbsp
Rock sugar to taste	
Salt to taste (optional)	
Dried black fungus (*hei mu er* /*mok yi*)	50 g, soaked and cleaned
Rice wine	250 ml (1 bowl)

- ✧ Clean chicken. Discard head, neck and legs. Trim off excess fat. Cut into average-size pieces.
- ✧ Combine all beans, peanuts, ginger and water in a saucepan. Simmer for 30 minutes or until beans split.
- ✧ Heat oil in a wok. Fry chicken pieces for a few minutes. Remove and add to beans. Add sugar and salt to taste. Simmer for 15–20 minutes. Add fungus. Simmer for 5 minutes more.
- ✧ Bring soup to the boil. Add wine. Remove from heat and serve hot.

Tip
- ❖ Soy and adzuki beans can be used instead of broad beans and hyacinth beans. Do not confuse adzuki beans (*chi xiao dou* / *chek siew dau*) with red adzuki beans (*hong dou* / *hung dau*).

THE FIFTIES AND BEYOND

Although the aphorism "life begins at 50" is often bandied about, those who have touched two score and ten years have to face the fact that they do not have the same energy levels as the younger generation. This is a time when wear and tear through the years can and does often take its toll in various uncomfortable ways.

Aches, pains and numbness in body parts; palpitations and chills; poor appetite and indigestion; general ill health and a feeling of tiredness and being rundown are often experienced. It also takes that much longer to recover from mild bouts of fever, coughs, colds, sore throats and minor infections.

Since the organs are not functioning at peak levels, biological processes become increasingly less efficient and old age ailments such as poor blood circulation, impotence, general debility, backache and poor vision are commonly experienced. Other ailments that plague people in this age group are rheumatic pains, shortness of breath, bone and joint aches, heartburn, insomnia, constant fatigue and lack of energy.

Women, in particular, have to face the disrupting symptoms that accompany menopause — sudden hot flashes, unexplainable mood swings, episodes of excessive sweating, depression, headaches and even skin changes. Feelings of anxiety and turmoil are attributed to the climactic point in life when menstrual flow becomes less regular and predictable and eventually ceases altogether.

While a proper balanced diet, rest and the right attitude towards growing old will contribute to health in old age, traditionalists who subscribe to curative and restorative powers of herbal tonics believe that growing old can be made that much easier and less daunting. Over and above good, old-fashioned chicken soup and lean meats enhanced with a host of herbs, there is also a particular list of tonics prescribed for senior citizens. Ginseng, the 'longevity plant', features prominently in this list. This herb, with its proven ability to correct disorders of the central nervous system, normalise blood pressure, increase resistance and strengthen almost the entire defense mechanism of the body, seems tailored towards relieving many of the ills of old age, including poor vision and deafness.

Apart from ginseng, other herbs that help to improve strength, banish impotence and relieve general debility should be frequently consumed. Recognised sources of health maintenance, cordyceps (*dong chong xia cao / tung chung cho*) restore energy, stimulate nerve centres and improve muscular tone; boxthorn fruit (*gou qi zi / gei chi*) improves vision; astragalus root (*huang qi / puk kei*) improves poor blood circulation and relieves fatigue; and dates revive failing vigour and vitality. Women, in particular, are wont to encounter gynaecological disorders, which can be alleviated through the twin power boosters, Chinese angelica (*dang gui / dong kwai*) and codonopsis root (*dang shen / dong sum*). Even everyday ingredients such as ginger and peppercorns can be successfully employed to banish such ailments as chills, winds, colds, bloating and indigestion.

Although most of the recipes in this section are meant solely for older members of the household, there are some that can also be imbibed by the younger adults. This has been indicated in the recipes where applicable.

Recipes

Main Meals

Soups:
1. Egg and mint leaf soup p.178
2. Peanuts with pig's tail p.178
3. Trotter with ginger and black beans p.179
4. Chicken feet and adzuki bean soup p.179
5. Six treasure chicken soup p.180
6. Chicken feet and black bean soup p.180

Dishes:
1. Stir-fried chicken with ginger and rice wine p.182
2. Chicken in rice wine p.182
3. Egg in ginger and rice wine p.183
4. Chicken with Chinese angelica and astragalus root p.183

Brews and Teas

Tonic brews:
1. Double-boiled pigeon with ginger and water chestnuts p.184
2. Lamb with Chinese angelica p.184
3. Double-boiled chicken with ginseng p.185
4. Double-boiled black chicken with astragalus root p.185
6. Double-boiled chicken with Chinese angelica and red dates p.185
5. Double-boiled bird's nest with ginseng p.186
7. Minced beef and ginger stew p.188
8. Double-boiled lamb with herbs p.188
9. Lamb and ginger stew p.190
10. Double-boiled ginseng and black chicken p.190

Teas:
1. Astragalus and codonopsis roots with black beans p.191

Soups

Egg and mint leaf soup

Serves 1–2

A bowl of this soup will relieve gas distension, heavy heartburn or an upset stomach, discomforts that often strike the elderly. The egg makes it easier to drink this otherwise sharp and bland concoction which does away with flavouring of any kind.

Water	500 ml (2 bowls)
Mint leaves	1 bowl, thoroughly washed and drained
Salt	$1/2$ tsp
Egg	1, well beaten

✧ Bring water to the boil in a saucepan. Add mint leaves and salt. Pour beaten egg slowly into boiling soup. Stir for 2 minutes. Remove from heat and serve.

Tip

❖ If you are preparing this soup without any tonic purpose in mind, you can add $1/4$ tsp pepper, 1 tsp sesame seed oil and garnish with chopped spring onions.

Peanuts with pig's tail

Serves 4–6

This dish, while somewhat greasy and not exactly appetising, is tolerated due to the belief of its ability to strengthen an overworked back or spine. It is good for the whole family.

Pig's tail	1, washed and drained
Peanuts (groundnuts)	200 g, washed and drained
Salt	$1/2$ tsp or more to taste
Water	2 l (8 bowls)

✧ Cut tail into smaller pieces if the butcher has not already done that for you. Wash and drain. If preferred, blanch in boiling water to remove excess grease before cooking.

✧ Combine all ingredients in a saucepan. Simmer for up to 3 hours or until peanuts are soft. Serve hot.

Tips

❖ If cooking for one, use $1/3$ of the tail and reduce water to 500 ml (2 bowls) and peanuts to 50 g.

❖ It is advisable to abstain from eating dishes with excess fat or grease. If there is a thick layer of oil or fat in any stew or soup, plunge a dozen ice cubes into the soup. Solidified fat or oil will adhere to the ice cubes, but remember to remove them immediately afterwards or they will start to melt and dilute the soup.

Trotter with ginger and black beans
Serves 4–6

This delicacy has double potency — the trotter strengthens the legs, while the black beans improve blood circulation. Trotter cooked in any form is a favourite with some people and this version can be eaten by younger adults too.

Pig's trotter (foreleg)	1, about 1½ kg
Sesame seed oil	2 Tbsp
Garlic	1 clove, crushed
Ginger	2 4-cm knobs, crushed and cut into smaller pieces
Black beans	150 g, toasted in a dry nonstick pan until jumping, then swirled under a running tap and drained
Light soy sauce	2 Tbsp
Salt	¾ tsp
Water	2 l (8 bowls)

- ✧ Clean trotter. Cut into large pieces. Blanch in boiling water for 10 minutes to remove grease. Drain.
- ✧ Heat sesame seed oil in a wok. Add garlic and ginger. Fry until fragrant. Add trotter and stir for 10 minutes.
- ✧ Transfer to a saucepan. Add beans, soy sauce, salt and water. Bring to the boil. Simmer over low heat for 2–3 hours. Serve hot.

Chicken feet and adzuki bean soup
Serves 4–6

Chek siew dau, also known as adzuki beans, look much like the more familiar red adzuki bean but has an additional black line along the centre of the seed scar. The beans clear wind and gas from the stomach, while the chicken feet help to strengthen weak legs, especially rheumatic ones. This is a nourishing soup suitable for the whole family, and more so for those frequently in contact with water, eg dishwashing.

Chicken feet	15–18
Garlic	1 clove, well crushed
Adzuki beans (chi xiao dou / chek siew dau)	200 g, washed and drained
Water	2 l (8 bowls)
Salt	½ tsp or more to taste

- ✧ To clean chicken feet, first strip off scaly skins. Discard talons. Rub well with salt. Wash several times and drain.
- ✧ Combine all ingredients in a pot. Bring to the boil. Simmer for 2–3 hours. Serve hot.

Six treasure chicken soup

Serves 4–6

Chicken with six treasured herbs — cnidium and astragalus roots, Chinese angelica, boxthorn fruit, red dates, and dried longan — make for a sum total of one heartening, healthy brew with a fragrant sweetness. It is good for not only the old, but also the whole family.

Chicken	1, about 1 kg
Chinese angelica (*dang gui* / *dong kwai*)	30 g
Boxthorn fruit (*gou qi zi* / *gei chi*)	2 heaped Tbsp, washed and drained
Dried red dates (*hong zao* / *hung cho*)	20, stones removed
Cnidium root (*chuan xiong* / *chuen kung*)	20 g
Astragalus root (*huang qi* / *puk kei*)	30 g
Dried longan flesh	30 g, washed and drained
Water	2 l (8 bowls)
Salt	1/2 tsp or more to taste

- ✧ Clean chicken. Trim off excess fat and gristle. Skin, then cut into large pieces.
- ✧ Combine all ingredients in a large saucepan. Simmer over low heat for 3–4 hours. Serve hot.

Chicken feet and black bean soup

Serves 4–6

Chicken feet are good for the legs, and black beans are good for the heart and improving blood circulation. Any member of the family can imbibe this excellent tonic.

Chicken feet	15–18
Black beans	200 g, toasted in a dry nonstick pan until jumping, then swirled under a running tap and drained
Salt	1/2 tsp or more to taste
Ginger	3-cm knob, sliced
Water	2 l (8 bowls)

- ✧ To clean chicken feet, first strip off scaly skins. Discard talons. Rub well with salt. Wash several times and drain.
- ✧ Combine all ingredients in a big saucepan. Bring to the boil. Simmer for 3–4 hours. Serve hot.

Stir-fried chicken with ginger and rice wine
Serves 1–2

This potent tonic requires a lot of ginger and strong rice wine, as well as a good appetite.
It is reputed to boost strength and vigour, as well as banish aches, pains and gases from the body.

Chicken	1, small, about ³/₄ kg; replaceable with 3 chicken thighs
Light soy sauce	1 Tbsp
Rice wine	250 ml (1 bowl)
Salt	¹/₂ tsp
Sesame seed oil	3 Tbsp
Young ginger	600 g, finely shredded
Garlic	1 clove, crushed and diced
Light soy sauce	1 Tbsp
Pepper to taste	

✧ If using whole chicken, discard head, neck and legs. Cut into average-size pieces. Marinate chicken in soy sauce, wine and salt for 30 minutes.

✧ Heat sesame seed oil in a wok. Add ginger. Fry until light brown. Add garlic. Fry for 1 minute more.

✧ Drain chicken pieces from marinade and add to wok. Fry over high heat for 5 minutes.

✧ Add marinade. Bring to the boil. Simmer for 5 minutes or until chicken is cooked. Serve hot. Add pepper to taste.

Chicken in rice wine
Serves 1–2

This very robust, frills- and fuss-free dish is meant to restore stamina and invigorate an aging body.
Try a full dose of this potent concoction at least once a week if you have an appetite for hearty
peasant fare. Use a free range chicken, but mind the bite if your teeth are on the weak side.
Use good quality rice wine for this dish and more ginger can be used if preferred.

Free range chicken	1, about 1 kg
Rice wine	1 l (4 bowls)
Ginger	4-cm knob, bruised

✧ Clean chicken. Discard head, neck and legs. Remove skin, excess fat and gristle.

✧ Combine all ingredients in a saucepan. Simmer over low heat for 2–3 hours or until liquid is halved. Serve hot.

Egg in ginger and rice wine
Serves 1–2

This dish helps to clear water and wind retention in the body and is especially effective in countering the chills that often afflict older people. This recipe is easier to prepare than the previous one.

Sesame seed oil	2 Tbsp
Young ginger	2 4-cm knobs, finely shredded
Eggs	2, well beaten
Rice wine	1 Tbsp; replaceable with brandy or Chinese cooking wine (*hua tiao / fa dew*)
Salt	1 pinch
Light soy sauce	1 tsp

✧ Heat sesame seed oil in a wok. Add ginger. Fry until fragrant. Add eggs. Toss with fried ginger. Add wine and bring to the boil. Add salt and soy sauce. Serve hot.

Chicken with Chinese angelica and astragalus root
Serves 1–2

This very potent dish relieves cramps, gas, chills and water retention in the body, eg legs and face. Women also eat this after menstruating. If preferred, eggs can be used instead of chicken. The latter is better cooked skinless. If retaining skin, reduce oil used by one tablespoon.

Chicken	¹/₂; replaceable with 2 chicken thighs
Chinese angelica (*dang gui / dong kwai*)	2–3 pieces
Astragalus root (*huang qi / puk kei*)	2–3 slices
Water	500 ml (2 bowls)
Sesame seed oil	2 Tbsp
Ginger	4-cm knob, crushed and finely sliced
Light soy sauce	1 Tbsp
Salt	¹/₂ tsp
Rice wine	1 Tbsp

✧ Clean chicken. Discard head, neck and legs. Skin, then cut into average-size pieces.

✧ Combine Chinese angelica, astragalus root and water in a saucepan. Simmer for 1–1¹/₂ hours or until liquid is halved. Set aside.

✧ Heat sesame seed oil in a wok. Add ginger. Fry until fragrant and light brown. Increase heat, add chicken pieces and stir a few times. Then, fry chicken over low heat for about 10 minutes, stirring continuously.

✧ Add soy sauce and salt. Increase heat again and pour herbal liquid over chicken. Boil for 5 minutes. Remove from heat and serve immediately with wine added to boiling dish.

Tonic brews

Double-boiled pigeon with ginger and water chestnuts
Serves 1–2

This stimulating brew is very warming for the body. It works to relieve general weakness and anaemia, especially in old age.

Pigeons	4–5, small	✧ Clean pigeons. Wash and drain. Pat dry with kitchen paper. Season with soy sauce, wine and salt. Set aside for 15–20 minutes.
Light soy sauce	1 tsp	
Rice wine	2 Tbsp	
Salt	1 pinch or more to taste	
Stock (preferably chicken)	1 l (4 bowls)	✧ Put pigeons into a double-boiler or heatproof (flameproof) bowl. Pour stock over pigeons. Add water chestnuts, ginger and peppercorns. Double-boil for 4 hours. Serve hot.
Water chestnuts	150 g, peeled and diced	
Young ginger	4-cm knob, sliced	
Peppercorns	$1/2$ tsp	

Lamb with Chinese angelica
Serves 4–6

This is an extremely rich and heating dish. Those who are predisposed towards internal heat should avoid this tonic. Otherwise, the recipe is excellent for chills and fatigue. Family members whose bodies are more *yin* influenced can each consume up to 200 mililitres, or $3/4$ of a bowl.

Cooking oil	2 Tbsp	✧ Heat oil in a wok. Fry soybean paste. Add lamb and ginger. Stir a few times. Add salt, Chinese angelica, mushrooms and water chestnuts. Stir.
Soybean paste (*dou jiang / dau cheong*)	2–3 Tbsp	
Lean lamb	500 g, cut into 2-cm cubes	
Ginger	4-cm knob, thinly sliced	
Salt	$1/2$ tsp	
Chinese angelica (*dang gui / dong kwai*)	15 g	✧ Transfer to clay pot or saucepan. Add water. Simmer over low heat for 2–3 hours or until meat is tender. When done, bring to the boil and add wine. Remove and serve.
Dried Chinese mushrooms	12–15, soaked to soften, stems removed and thinly sliced	
Water chestnuts	20, peeled and halved	
Water	1 l (4 bowls)	
Rice wine	2 Tbsp	

Double-boiled chicken with ginseng

Serves 1–2

Ginseng has been documented as having the ability, among a host of others, to retard the degenerative process of aging. A free range chicken is recommended for this recipe.

Chicken	1, small, about $^3/_4$ kg; replaceable with 3 chicken thighs	✧ Combine all ingredients in a double-boiler or heatproof (flameproof) bowl. Double-boil for 4 hours. Drink warm.
Water	750 ml (3 bowls)	
Ginseng	25 g	
Salt	$^1/_2$ tsp	

Double-boiled black chicken with astragalus root

Serves 1–2

This soup aids blood circulation and promotes good health.

Black chicken	1	✧ Combine all ingredients in a double-boiler or heatproof (flameproof) bowl. Double-boil for 4 hours. Drink warm.
Astragalus root (*huang qi / puk kei*)	30 g	
Water	$^1/_2$ l (2 bowls)	

Double-boiled chicken with Chinese angelica and red dates

Serves 4–6

Although this brew is excellent for the whole family, it is especially recommended for relieving menopausal symptoms such as spasms, hot flashes and sweating.

Chicken	1, about 1 kg	✧ Combine all ingredients in a double-boiler or heatproof (flameproof) bowl. Double-boil for 4 hours. Drink warm.
Chinese angelica (*dang gui / dong kwai*)	35 g	
Dried red dates (*hong zao / hung cho*)	20–25, stones removed	
Water	1–1$^1/_2$ l (4–6 bowls)	

Double-boiled bird's nest with ginseng

Serves 1–2

This is best imbibed by the elderly, especially those weakened and devitalised after prolonged illness. Herbalists are generally wary about giving ginseng to children or young adults. As cooled bird's nest can be kept refrigerated, do not feel compelled to consume all of this brew at one go. Have, perhaps, one bowl in the morning, one in the evening and the last, the following morning.

Bird's nest	20 g
Ginseng	10–15 g
Water	1 l (4 bowls)
Rock sugar	80 g

✧ Preparing bird's nest is a time-consuming and tedious chore unless you opt for the prepacked ones that have already been cleaned of impurities. If not, you have to soak bird's nest for 3–4 hours in cold water before picking out impurities such as tiny feathers and twigs with a pair of new or similarly clean tweezers. Soak a second time to loosen any remaining impurities. Rinse and drain.

✧ Combine all ingredients in a double-boiler or heatproof (flameproof) bowl. Double-boil for 4 hours. At the end of the cooking time, remove cover and wipe dry to prevent condensation droplets from dripping into soup. Leave to cool a while, then drink warm.

Minced beef and ginger stew

Serves 4–6

Those with arthritic or rheumatic legs may find some relief through this curative brew, which is heating and nourishing. It is also excellent for family members predisposed to *yin* energy and related ailments.

Minced fresh lean beef	500 g
Garlic	1 clove, crushed
Ginger	4-cm knob, finely sliced
Water	1 l (4 bowls)
Salt	1 pinch

✧ Combine all ingredients in a saucepan. Simmer over low heat for 2–3 hours or until liquid is halved. Drink hot.

Tip

✧ For thicker beef tea, which is delightfully delicious, double-boil the beef. First, put an inverted heatproof (flameproof) bowl into a bigger, upright heatproof bowl. Then, put beef on top of the upturned bowl. Cover the bigger bowl with a snug-fitting lid and put the whole setup into a saucepan of boiling water. Cover the saucepan and double-boil for 3–4 hours. Every half hour, add 1 Tbsp water to the meat to prevent it from sticking to the bowl or drying out. You will get about 500 ml (2 bowls) of thick, nourishing beef tea. Drink hot. For an even more potent tonic, add 2 pieces of Chinese angelica (*dang gui / dong kwai*) to the beef before double-boiling.

Double-boiled lamb with herbs

Serves 4–6

Local fresh lamb is usually considered more nutritious for double-boiling than frozen cuts. Drink the soup hot because it will give off a strong smell as it cools and fat starts to coagulate at the surface.

Minced fresh lamb	600 g
Astragalus root (*huang qi / puk kei*)	20 g
Chinese angelica (*dang gui / dong kwai*)	20 g
Boxthorn fruit (*gou qi zi / gei chi*)	2 heaped tsp
Dried black dates (*hei zao / hak cho*)	8–10, stones removed
Water	500–750 ml (2–3 bowls)

✧ Combine all ingredients in a double-boiler or heatproof (flameproof) bowl. Double-boil for 4 hours. Drink hot before going to bed.

Lamb and ginger stew
Serves 4–6

Although high in fat content, lamb has always been regarded as nourishing, very heating and extremely effective in combating jaded spirits, exhaustion, low energy levels and general debility. This stew is highly recommended to those suffering from or susceptible to anaemia and chills. Those whose bodies are already more *yang* inclined should refrain from this dish to avoid overheating or they may suffer from nose bleeds. People with fevers, colds and influenza also should not eat lamb.

Fresh lean lamb	500 g, cut into 2-cm cubes
Garlic	1 clove, crushed
Water	1 l (4 bowls)
Ginger	4-cm knob, finely sliced
Salt	1 pinch

Tip
❖ Those who want a thicker, richer and tastier brew can, alternatively, double-boil the lamb. Omit the 1 l water and mince the lamb instead. Then, double-boil as described on p.188 for 4–5 hours. You will get about 500 ml (2 bowls) of liquid.

✧ Fry lamb and garlic in a dry wok for a few minutes to remove any excess fat or smell.
✧ Combine water, ginger and fried lamb and garlic in a saucepan. Simmer over low heat for 2–3 hours or until liquid is halved. Drink hot.

Double-boiled ginseng and black chicken
Serves 1–2

This is an excellent tonic for the anaemic. It not only helps the body's metabolism, but also strengthens the body's defence mechanism. Adults or young children suffering from a debility usually drink a few spoonfuls of this rich brew to aid recovery.

Black chicken	1, head and legs removed
Ginseng	20 g
Water	1/2 l (2 bowls)

✧ Combine all ingredients in a double-boiler or heatproof (flameproof) bowl. Double-boil for 4 hours. Drink warm.

Astragalus and codonopsis roots with black beans

Serves 4–6

Combining astragalus and codonopsis roots makes an effective remedy in countering lethargy, and black beans improve blood circulation, making this a rejuvenating and energising tea. It is particularly effective for those who have a million and two things to do in a 24-hour day and suffer from extreme fatigue at the end of the day. The tea is a soothing blend that tastes like a red bean dessert, only smoother and without any crunch unless you eat the beans too.

Astragalus root (*huang qi / puk kei*)	30 g
Codonopsis root (*dang shen / dong sum*)	30 g
Black beans	200 g, toasted in a dry nonstick pan until jumping, then swirled under a running tap and drained
Water	2–3 l (8–12 bowls)

✧ Combine all ingredients in a big saucepan. Simmer at least 4 hours. Drink warm 2–3 times a day.

___

Tip

❖ If you simmer for less than 4 hours, you might get a slight 'beany' taste in the tea, which indicates that the beans are not cooked thoroughly.

AIDS FOR COMMON ILLS

While the preceding sections of this book contain some recipes for curative fare, they have mainly featured preventive and nutritive dishes, and for specific age groups or purposes. This section is devoted to addressing the more common health problems of both young and old such as sore throats, nausea, nosebleeds, overheating bodies and mild diarrhoea. Although it is important for those suffering from general weakness or recovering from a long illness to be put on a nourishing diet, care has to be exercised that this is done within reason — too much of a good thing can be bad and defeat the original purpose of aiding recovery. An overdose of herbal or tonic foods, while not likely to be fatal, can overburden a weak body.

Generally, those who are of a weak constitution or have intestinal or digestive problems should go easy on herbal brews, soups or drinks. Such individuals need a longer time to attune their bodies to the potentially overpowering effects of herbal concoctions. Mending parts of the body, like the heart, through tonic nutrition takes time and the pace is slow. This applies to both children and adults. Also, one should never start imbibing strong tonic brews immediately after a long illness, serious disease or major surgery. Instead, allow a week or two before starting with minimal doses of strengthening brews and building up over an extended period of time to enable the body to adapt, accept and accommodate new and effective inputs.

Although they have been tried and tested through generations, the following ways of alleviating common ills are by no means the be all and end all of cures. In the final analysis, commonsense has to prevail. It is very well to take a dose of ginger water to relieve bloatedness and abdominal pain but if the pains are chronic and severe, no amount of ginger juice will eradicate a condition that calls for medical help or even hospitalisation. That goes, too, for severe cases of diarrhoea that cannot be remedied with a bowl or two of barley or rice gruel. Furthermore, if you are having a bad cough or cold, wait until these conditions clear up before drinking any potent brew. In the case of children, knowledgeable mothers never give their very young children potent brews, especially those involving Chinese ginseng, for fear of stunting their children's growth or making them suffer from cramps or spasms due to adverse effects on their central nervous systems.

❄ All recipes in this section make one serving, except for *Dried abalone with herbs*. Some recipes involve large amounts because they (usually tonics, brews and teas) are to be imbibed several times a day to optimise the effects. To keep warm, store in thermos flasks, but be sure to finish drinking it before the end of the day.

❄ Unless specified otherwise, the concoctions in this section should be imbibed two to three times a week, and they should be prepared fresh each time. Once you feel the positive effects, discontinue.

❄ Unless directed otherwise, the concoctions should be taken at the onset or early stage of the illness.

❄ Unless mentioned otherwise, the recipes in this section are suitable only for those aged eight and older.

Recipes

1. To heal superficial wounds, bruises and cuts quickly: Catfish, kudzu shoot and pork rib soup p.196
2. To help stitches heal faster after operations: Catfish herbal brew p.196
3. To relieve boils and ulcers in the mouth: Rice tea p.198
4. To relieve a hoarse, dry throat: Chinese pear in salt p.198
5. To relieve a hoarse, heated throat: Watermelon with honey p.198
6. To relieve a sore throat: Cucumber core p.199
7. To soothe internal heat: Chinese pear with red dates and rock sugar p.199
8. To remove chills and humidity in adults: Double-boiled pigeon soup p.199
9. To cure cold coughs: Ginger and black date tea p.200
10. To relieve heated cough and hoarseness: Onion juice and honey p.200
11. To cure heated coughs: Mint leaf and honey tea p.200
12. For relieving insomnia in adults: Dried abalone and lean pork soup p.202
13. To relieve nosebleeds: Steamed catfish p.202
14. To cure nosebleeds: Catfish with black beans p.202
15. To relieve congestion or stomach gas and also clear phlegm from throat: Onion drink p.203
16. To stop nausea, vomiting and gas distension or gas cramps in the stomach: Mint tea p.203
17. To clear female white discharge: Pig's tripe with gingko nuts p.203
18. To relieve a prolonged dry, hacking cough: Watercress with sweet dates and sugared melon strips p.204
19. To relieve stomach and intestinal irritation: Pearl barley water and milk p.204
20. To relieve gas distension, gas cramps and to stimulate a poor appetite: Ginger tea p.204
21. To relieve migraines and headaches: *Pau sum* ginseng tea p.206
22. To relieve headaches or high blood pressure: Pig's brain and green apples p.206
23. To alleviate discomfort of measles in children: Carrot and water chestnut tea p.206
24. To heal and restore the body after a serious illness: Double-boiled baby pigeons with herbs p.207
25. To alleviate anaemia: Hasima and red dates p.207
26. For immediate relief from digestive upsets:
    a) Raw lotus root juice p.208
    b) Steamed lotus root juice with red dates and rock sugar p.208
27. To combat burnout, intense work stress and extreme fatigue in adults: Dried abalone with herbs p.208
28. To combat the ravages of old age: Chinese pear and pork rib soup p.210
29. To restore strength and vitality after operations, also to build health of children: Chicken essence p.210
30. To relieve excessive sweating in babies and young children: White atractylodes and Chinese yam tea p.212
31. To alleviate diabetes:
    a) Roseapple tea p.212
    b) Chinese yam and boxthorn fruit tea p.212
32. To combat loss of appetite: Frog's leg and astragalus root soup p.214
33. To cure incontinence in young children: Gecko with lean pork p.214

To heal superficial wounds, bruises and cuts quickly:

Catfish, kudzu shoot and pork rib soup

Serves 1

Known in Cantonese as *got choy*, kudzu shoots are available fresh mostly in wet markets and are rarely sold in supermakets. If you cannot get them, substitute with 35 grams of Solomon's seal (*yu zhu / yok chok*).

Cooking oil	2–3 Tbsp	✧ Heat oil in a wok. Add fish and fry with ginger. Remove from wok and set aside.
Catfish	1, average-size; gutted, cleaned and cut into 2–3 pieces	
Ginger	4-cm knob, crushed	✧ Combine all ingredients, including fried fish and kudzu roots, in a pot. Simmer over low heat for $1^1/_2$–2 hours. Serve only soup.
Pork ribs	100 g, cut into small pieces	
Kudzu shoots	125 g, washed, cut into large pieces and roots reserved	
Water	750–1000 ml (3–4 bowls)	
Salt to taste		

To help stitches heal faster after operations:

Catfish herbal brew

Serves 1

Stitches are believed to mend and heal faster if this brew is consumed, but only twice in all and not more than once a week. More than that and unsightly excessive skin growth will occur where the stitches are healing.

Catfish	1, about $^1/_2$ kg; gutted, cleaned and cut into large pieces	✧ Combine all ingredients in a saucepan. Simmer for 3–4 hours. Drink soup warm throughout the day.
Astragalus root (*huang qi / puk kei*)	35 g	
Solomon's seal (*yu zhu / yok chok*)	35 g	
Codonopsis root (*dang shen / dong sum*)	35 g	
Water	2 l (8 bowls)	

To relieve boils and ulcers in the mouth:

Rice tea

Serves 1

It is more practical and economical to prepare this tea when cooking rice.

✧ Add 500 ml (2 bowls) extra water to rice when cooking for family. When contents of rice cooker or pot is bubbling and boiling, scoop out about 1½ bowls of liquid. Leave to cool a while, then sip warm throughout the day in place of water.

To relieve a hoarse, dry throat:

Chinese pear in salt

Serves 1

The pear used here is known in Cantonese as *shuet lei* or "snow pear", which is the small, mottled variety and yellow in colour.

Chinese pears	3, peeled, halved and cored	✧ Combine pears and water in a pot. Simmer for 3–4 hours. Add water if excessive evaporation takes place. Remove from heat. Add salt. Drink warm.
Water	750 ml (3 bowls)	
Salt	1 pinch	

To relieve a hoarse, heated throat:

Watermelon with honey

Serves 1

Fresh watermelon	2–3 slices	✧ Spoon honey over watermelon or dip watermelon slices into honey and eat.
Pure honey	1–2 Tbsp	

To relieve a sore throat:

Cucumber core
Serves 1

Cucumber	½	✧ Extract core of the cucumber.
Salt	1 tsp	Dip core in salt and eat.

To soothe internal heat:

Chinese pear with red dates and rock sugar
Serves 1

The pears used here are Chinese pears, known as *sui cheng lei* or "crystal pears" in Cantonese. They are round and yellow in colour.

Chinese pears	2, peeled, halved and cored	✧ Except for rock sugar, combine all other ingredients in a pot. Simmer
Dried red dates (*hong zao* / *hung cho*)	6–8, stones removed	for 3–4 hours. Add more rock sugar and/or water to taste if
Water	750 ml (3 bowls)	necessary. Drink warm.
Rock sugar	100 g	

To remove chills and humidity in adults:

Double-boiled pigeon soup
Serves 1

This is an excellent prescription for many ills, among them, general physical weakness, irregular menstruation and even asthma. It removes chills and humidity from the body and tonifies the blood. It is very 'heaty' and those who cannot take warming or stimulating soups should not try it. The dosage here is suitable only for adults. If giving to adolescents or younger children (at least eight years of age) dispense only one to two tablespoons at a time.

Pigeons	2, cleaned and with head, neck and legs removed	✧ Combine all ingredients in a double-boiler or heatproof (flameproof) dish. Double-boil for
Ginger	4-cm knob, sliced	4 hours. Serve soup hot and only 250 ml (1 bowl). Reserve other bowl in a thermos flask
Fresh young ginger	4-cm knob, thinly sliced	and serve 4–5 hours later.
Peppercorns	1 tsp	✧ Alternatively, combine all ingredients in a pot
Garlic	1 clove, crushed	with 250 ml (1 bowl) more water. Simmer for
Water	500 ml (2 bowls)	3–4 hours or until liquid is reduced to ⅔ of original amount. Serve as above.

To cure cold coughs (from too much iced or cold drinks):

Ginger and black date tea

Serves 1

Young ginger	3 thick slices, bruised
Dried black dates	
(*hei zao* / *hak cho*)	7, stones removed
Water	250 ml (1 bowl)

✧ Combine all ingredients in a clay pot. Simmer over charcoal heat for 30 minutes or until liquid is reduced to about 200 ml ($^3/_4$ bowl). Drink warm.

Tip

✧ For all types of coughs, it helps to gargle with lukewarm salt water 2–3 times a day.

To relieve heated cough and hoarseness:

Onion juice and honey

Serves 1

Onion juice	extracted from 6–8 onions
Pure honey	1–2 Tbsp
Hot water	1 tsp

✧ Mix onion juice with honey. Add water to combine into a smooth consistency. If too thick, add more water.

✧ Swallow 1 tsp at a time, 4 times a day and at intervals of 1–2 hours until throat condition improves.

To cure heated coughs (from too much heating or spicy food):

Mint leaf and honey tea

Serves 1

Mint leaves	10–12, well washed
Warm water	1 Tbsp
Honey	1 Tbsp

✧ Extract about 1 tsp juice from mint leaves. Add warm water and honey. Sip concoction.

For relieving insomnia in adults:

Dried abalone and lean pork soup

Serves 1

This recipe is more effective when high-grade abalone is used.

Dried abalone	1, washed and soaked in 375 ml (1½ bowls) water overnight	◇ Combine abalone, soaking liquid and lean pork in a saucepan. Simmer over low heat for 2–3 hours. Eat abalone pieces. Drink liquid before going to bed.
Lean pork	150 g, thickly sliced	

To relieve nosebleeds:

Steamed catfish

Serves 1

Catfish is believed to be a great aid in blood clotting. Omit ginger or pepper as these will make the dish 'heaty' and aggravate nosebleeds further. Those very prone to nosebleeds can eat this dish once a week.

Catfish	1, about ½ kg; gutted and cleaned	◇ Rub fish all over with salt.
Salt	1–2 tsp	◇ Arrange catfish on a heatproof (flameproof) dish. Sprinkle spring onions and ½ tsp salt on top. Steam for 15–20 minutes until cooked.
Spring onions (scallions)	3–4 stalks, chopped	

To cure nosebleeds:

Catfish with black beans

Serves 1

This is a traditional brew prescribed for people who suffer from nosebleeds due to overheated internal systems or the excessive consumption of potent tonic herbs.

Catfish	1, average-size; gutted and cleaned	◇ Rub fish all over with salt to remove grime. Wash off salt and drain well.
Salt	1–2 Tbsp	◇ Heat oil in a wok. Add ginger and fish. Fry for 2 minutes. Remove from wok and set aside.
Cooking oil	2–3 Tbsp	◇ Combine fried fish and ginger, black beans and water in a pot. Simmer over low heat for 1½–2 hours. Serve only soup. Although this dish is supposed to be consumed without salt, adding a pinch to taste is harmless.
Ginger	4-cm knob, crushed	
Black beans	125 g, toasted in a dry nonstick pan until jumping, then swirled under a running tap and drained	
Water	750 ml (3 bowls)	

To relieve congestion or stomach gas and also clear phlegm from throat:

Onion drink

Serves 1

Onions	6–8, peeled, washed and thinly sliced
Boiling water	250 ml (1 bowl)

✧ Put onions into a porcelain container with a lid. Add boiling water and cover. Leave to cool, then sip throughout the day.

Tip

❖ For those who find the drink too strong, try onion gruel instead. Prepare as above, then strain and add liquid to cooked porridge, rice or milk. This concoction will help towards a good night's restful sleep.

To stop nausea, vomiting and gas distension or gas cramps in the stomach:

Mint tea

Serves 1

Mint leaves	1 bowlful, well washed and drained
Boiling water	500 ml (2 bowls)

✧ Put mint leaves into a pot. Add boiling water. Leave to stand for 5–10 minutes. Strain off leaves. Drink warm 3–4 times throughout the day.

To clear female white discharge:

Pig's tripe with gingko nuts

Serves 1

Pig's tripe	1, small; thoroughly cleaned (refer to p.109)
Water	1¹/₂ l (6 bowls)
Salt	1 tsp
Peppercorns (optional)	1 Tbsp
Gingko nuts (*bai guo / bak gor*)	40–50, shelled

✧ Combine pig's tripe, water, salt and peppercorns if used in a saucepan. Cover and simmer for 1–1¹/₂ hours. Add gingko nuts 45 minutes before removing from heat. Drink soup hot throughout the day.

To relieve a prolonged dry, hacking cough:

Watercress with sweet dates and sugared melon strips

Serves 1

Whereas the larger species of watercress is used for soups at mealtimes, you have to use the smaller species in this soup as the former is too cooling. Drink this soup once a week for two or three weeks. Prepare this brew fresh each time.

Watercress (*si yang cai / sai yong choy*)	250 g, washed and roots discarded
Sweet dates (*mi zao / mut cho*)	15–20, stones removed
Sugared winter melon strips	6–8
Water	1 l (4 bowls)

✧ Combine all ingredients in a saucepan. Simmer over low heat for 2–3 hours or until liquid is halved. Drink warm before going to bed.

To relieve stomach and intestinal irritation (but not for diarrhoea as milk will aggravate the condition):

Pearl barley water and milk

Serves 1

Pearl barley	25 g, washed and drained
Water	1 l (4 bowls)
Sugared winter melon strips	6–8
Rock sugar	50 g
Milk	500 ml (2 bowls)

✧ Except for rock sugar and milk, combine all other ingredients in a saucepan. Boil for 45 minutes. Add sugar. Boil for 10–15 minutes more. Remove from heat.

✧ Combine 125 ml ($^1/_2$ bowl) barley liquid with 60 ml milk or according to consistency preferred. Drink warm several times a day.

To relieve gas distension, gas cramps, and to stimulate a poor appetite:

Ginger tea

Serves 1

Fresh ginger	2 4-cm knobs, crushed and thickly sliced
Dried red dates (*hong zao / hung cho*)	6, stones removed
Water	375 ml (1$^1/_2$ bowls)

✧ Combine all ingredients in a pot. Simmer for about 1$^1/_2$ hours or until liquid is reduced. Drain and squeeze dates for liquid to return to pot. Discard pulp. Strain, then drink once or twice a day.

To relieve migraines and headaches:

Pau sum ginseng tea

Serves 1

Pau sum ginseng	30 g
Water	2 l (8 bowls)

✧ Combine ingredients in a double-boiler or heatproof (flameproof) bowl. Double-boil for 4 hours.

✧ Alternatively, add 125 ml ($^1/_2$ bowl) more water and simmer over low heat for 3 hours. Leave to cool and stand overnight (not in the refrigerator). Drink in the morning before leaving for work or school.

To relieve headaches and high blood pressure:

Pig's brain and green apples

Serves 1

Pig's brain	1, thoroughly cleaned (refer to p.90)
Green apples	2, washed, cored and cut into quarters
Water	375 ml (1$^1/_2$ bowls)

✧ Combine all ingredients in a saucepan. Simmer over low heat for 3–4 hours. Drink warm. Add salt to taste if preferred.

To alleviate discomfort of measles in children:

Carrot and water chestnut tea

Serves 1

Carrot	1, grated
Water chestnuts	4–5, peeled
Water	750 ml (3 bowls)

✧ Combine all ingredients in a pot. Simmer over low heat until liquid is halved. Drink warm 3 times a day, 125 ml ($^1/_2$ bowl) at a time, and at 2 hourly intervals. Repeat for 3–4 days.

To heal and restore the body after a serious illness:

Double-boiled baby pigeons with herbs
Serves 1

This rich and potent brew is much favoured by the elderly. It is said to be very strengthening and has amazing healing properties for those who are recovering from serious illnesses, accidents or burns. This recipe was given to me by a friend. His cousin had suffered severe burns from a gas explosion, as well as long-term shock and trauma. The cousin was put on a diet of this tonic and recovered well enough to lead a normal life.

2- or 3-day-old pigeons	2–3; the birds used can be older but should not yet have any feathers	✧ Clean pigeons. Wash well and drain. Remove innards as best you can without having to wash pigeons a second time.
Chinese yam (*shan yao / wai san*)	30 g	✧ Combine all ingredients in a heatproof (flameproof) dish. Double-boil for up to 4 hours. Drink brew before going to bed.
Astragalus root (*huang qi / puk kei*)	30 g	✧ Alternatively, pound pigeons until fine. Add boiling water, then squeeze out liquid. Double-boil liquid for up to 2 hours. Drink warm before going to bed.
Water	250 ml (1 bowl)	

To alleviate anaemia:

Hasima and red dates
Serves 1

Omit *pau sum* ginseng if you do not like the taste.

Hasima (*xue ge / shuet kup*)	50–60 g, veins removed, soaked for 1 hour, then well drained	✧ Combine all ingredients in a pot. Simmer for 3–4 hours. Serve hot or cold.
Dried red dates (*hong zao / hung cho*)	20, stones removed	
Gingko nuts (*bai guo / bak gor*)	30, shelled	
Precooked lotus seeds	50	
Pau sum ginseng	4–6 pieces	
Rock sugar	100 g	
Screwpine (*pandan*) leaves (optional)	2, knotted together	
Water	2 l (8 bowls)	

For immediate relief from digestive upsets, eg indigestion from eating rich foods:

a. Raw lotus root juice

(for those with strong stomachs)

Lotus root	1/2, grated	✧ Extract 1–2 Tbsp juice from grated lotus root. Drink immediately.

b. Steamed lotus root juice with red dates and rock sugar

(for those with sensitive digestive systems)

Raw lotus root juice	3–4 Tbsp, extracted from 1 length of lotus root, grated	✧ Combine all ingredients in a heatproof (flameproof) bowl. Steam for 30 minutes. Remove.
Dried red dates (*hong zao / hung cho*)	6, stones removed	✧ Sip warm, 60 ml (1/4 bowl) at a time at intervals of 10–15 minutes.
Water	250 ml (1 bowl)	
Rock sugar (optional)	1 small piece	

To combat burnout, intense work stress and extreme fatigue in adults:

Dried abalone with herbs

Serves 3

This very effective and rejuvenating tonic is not only expensive, but also very tedious to prepare, taking up to three days in all. The positive results, however, are well worth it.

Dried abalone	2 pieces, cleaned and soaked in 375 ml (3 bowls) water overnight	✧ Combine soaked abalone, soaking liquid and cordyceps in a slow cooker. Leave to simmer overnight.
Cordyceps (*dong chong xia cao / tung chung cho*)	30 g	✧ The following morning, add boxthorn fruit, dates and chicken. Continue simmering until evening. Drink soup before going to bed.
Boxthorn fruit (*gou qi zi / gei chi*)	2 heaped Tbsp	
Dried red dates (*hong zao / hung cho*)	10–12, stones removed	
Chicken breast	1, replaceable with 2 drumsticks, skinned and fat trimmed	

Tip

✧ If you want a less time-consuming way of preparing this restorative dish, soak the abalone in water overnight. The next morning, combine all ingredients in a slow cooker or saucepan. Simmer for 3–4 hours. Drink soup before going to bed.

To combat the ravages of old age:

Chinese pear and pork rib soup

Serves 1

Some people regard this potion as the elixir of youth. Prepare it once or twice a week.

Chinese pears (*xue li / shuet lei*)	3–4, peeled and cored
Pork ribs	200 g, fat trimmed
Water	1 l (4 bowls)

✧ Combine all ingredients in a pot. Simmer for 3–4 hours. Drink soup warm as you would water throughout the day.

Tip

❖ If you wish to simmer this soup over charcoal heat, add 250 ml (1 bowl) more water.

To restore strength and vitality after operations, also to build health of children:

Chicken essence

Serves 1

This recipe makes pure chicken essence, which restores vitality and strength after operations among other things (imbibe only three to four weeks after the operation). The brew is also suitable for children, who will gain better health consuming just a couple of spoonfuls at a time. It can also be taken once a week when feeling rundown.

Free range chicken	1, ³/₄–1 kg; cleaned and skinned

✧ Pound chicken until bones break. Put atop an inverted heatproof (flameproof) bowl. Place inverted bowl into a larger heatproof bowl. Cover and double-boil for 6 hours over charcoal heat. Drink warm.

To relieve excessive sweating in babies and young children:

White atractylodes and Chinese yam tea
Serves 1

This tea is said to relieve excessive sweating in babies, especially those prone to it even on cool days. Babies between six and 10 months old should be given small dosages only, about one to two teaspoonfuls at a time.

White atractylodes	
(*bai zhu / bak surt*)	10 g
Chinese yam	
(*shan yao / wai san*)	10 g
Water	250 ml (1 bowl)

- Combine all ingredients in a saucepan. Simmer for 1–1¹/₂ hours or until liquid changes colour and has reduced by about half. Leave to cool.
- Mix a little of the liquid with baby's milk. Reserve the rest for baby's other feeds.

To alleviate diabetes

Serves 1

There are several tonic remedies prescribed for diabetes. Some sufferers find the following two recipes helpful in relieving certain symptoms, which include great thirst, weakness and emaciation due to lack of sugar in the blood.

a. Roseapple tea

Jambu is the Malay name of this pink, waxy-skinned fruit. For this recipe, use the smaller variety, which have lots of seeds, and not the bigger, fleshier cross-bred type. This tea can be drunk twice a week.

Roseapples	4–5, medium-size; wiped with clean cloth and left whole and unpeeled
Water	1 l (4 bowls)

- Combine ingredients in a slow cooker or saucepan. Simmer for 8–12 hours. If simmering in a saucepan, add water from time to time to prevent drying out. Discard pulp. Drink tea warm 2–3 times a day.

b. Chinese yam and boxthorn fruit tea.

These two herbs are believed to effectively regulate or reduce blood sugar levels. Those averse to tonic aromas may add a cut of very lean meat to the brew to make it a soup. This tea can be consumed once a week.

Chinese yam	
(*shan yao / wai san*)	50 g
Boxthorn fruit	
(*gou qi zi / gei chi*)	50 g
Water	1 l (4 bowls)

- Combine all ingredients in a saucepan. Simmer for 3–4 hours. Drain and discard Chinese yam, but boxthorn fruit can be eaten if desired. Drink tea warm, 2–3 times a day.

To combat loss of appetite:

Frog's leg and astragalus root soup

Serves 1

This is given to children to maintain a good appetite or to restore appetite loss.

Frog's legs	6–8, medium-size
Astragalus root	
(*huang qi* / *puk kei*)	35 g
Water	1 l (4 bowls)
Salt	1/2 tsp

- ◇ Frog's legs sold in wet markets are usually already cleaned and skinned. Before cooking, cut each into two at knee joint. Remove veins, then wash well under running water.
- ◇ Combine all ingredients in a saucepan. Simmer for 4 hours. Drain and discard solid ingredients. Drink soup warm.

Tip

- ❖ If using a cooking method that incurs little to no evaporation, reduce water by 250 ml (1 bowl).

To cure incontinence in young children:

Gecko with lean pork

Serves 1

With a less than flattering common name, gecko here refers to *Gekko gecko (Linnaeus)*, a species that is known to herbalists as having the ability to address incontinence by strengthening one's kidneys. Tried and tested with success by my friends on their children, this recipe has to be taken once every two weeks until it takes effect, after which, discontinue. For pork, choose as lean a cut as possible. Pork is preferred to chicken as some consider chicken too heating. The salt is to mask the smell and taste of the brew.

Gecko (*ge jie* / *kup kwai*)	1 pair (male and female)
Lean pork	200 g
Water	750 ml (3 bowls)
Salt	1/2 tsp

- ◇ Combine all ingredients in a saucepan. Simmer for 3–4 hours or until liquid is halved. Drink liquid only.

Weights & Measures

Quantities for this book are given in Metric and American (spoon and cup) measures. Standard spoon and cup measurements used are:

1 teaspoon = 5 ml, 1 dessertspoon = 10 ml, 1 tablespoon = 15 ml, 1 cup = 250 ml. All measures are level unless otherwise stated.

LIQUID AND VOLUME MEASURES

Metric	Imperial	American
5 ml	$^1/_6$ fl oz	1 teaspoon
10 ml	$^1/_3$ fl oz	1 dessertspoon
15 ml	$^1/_2$ fl oz	1 tablespoon
60 ml	2 fl oz	$^1/_4$ cup (4 tablespoons)
85 ml	$2^1/_2$ fl oz	$^1/_3$ cup
90 ml	3 fl oz	$^3/_8$ cup (6 tablespoons)
125 ml	4 fl oz	$^1/_2$ cup
180 ml	6 fl oz	$^3/_4$ cup
250 ml	8 fl oz	1 cup
300 ml	10 fl oz ($^1/_2$ pint)	$1^1/_4$ cups
375 ml	12 fl oz	$1^1/_2$ cups
435 ml	14 fl oz	$1^3/_4$ cups
500 ml	16 fl oz	2 cups
625 ml	20 fl oz (1 pint)	$2^1/_2$ cups
750 ml	24 fl oz ($1^1/_5$ pints)	3 cups
1 liter	32 fl oz ($1^3/_5$ pints)	4 cups
1.25 liters	40 fl oz (2 pints)	5 cups
1.5 liters	48 fl oz ($2^2/_5$ pints)	6 cups
2.5 liters	80 fl oz (4 pints)	10 cups

DRY MEASURES

Metric	Imperial
30 grams	1 ounce
45 grams	$1^1/_2$ ounces
55 grams	2 ounces
70 grams	$2^1/_2$ ounces
85 grams	3 ounces
100 grams	$3^1/_2$ ounces
110 grams	4 ounces
125 grams	$4^1/_2$ ounces
140 grams	5 ounces
280 grams	10 ounces
450 grams	16 ounces (1 pound)
500 grams	1 pound, $1^1/_2$ ounces
700 grams	$1^1/_2$ pounds
800 grams	$1^3/_4$ pounds
1 kilogram	2 pounds, 3 ounces
1.5 kilograms	3 pounds, $4^1/_2$ ounces
2 kilograms	4 pounds, 6 ounces

LENGTH

Metric	Imperial
0.5 cm	$^1/_4$ inch
1 cm	$^1/_2$ inch
1.5 cm	$^3/_4$ inch
2.5 cm	1 inch

ABBREVIATION

Tbsp	tablespoon
tsp	teaspoon
kg	kilogram
g	gram
l	liters
ml	milliliters
oz	ounce
lb	pound